THE

MIRACLE

www.houseofpapaj.com

IS

YOU

BY JEFFREY J. HALPERIN

AKA

PAPA J

Jeffrey J. Halperin

www.houseofpapaj.com

PSSSST! Hey you! Yeah, you!
Got a Minute?

Come here for a moment.
I have something to tell you!
It's a secret, though, so you can't tell anyone else!
Now listen up real close.
YOU ARE GREAT!
Did you hear that?
Well didja?
Yeah, you got it right.
YOU ARE REALLY GREAT!
 I am not lying. Really, I can prove it to you. Will you take a few
minutes out of your busy day and listen?

Here's another one! Not only are YOU GREAT, but

YOU ARE ALSO A MIRACLE!

Yeah, YOU ARE A MIRACLE. You heard me right.
In fact, I'll tell you something else, too.
Are you ready for this?

YOU CAN PERFORM MIRACLES.

HAH! How about that one?
Don't laugh; it's true.

TURN THE PAGE!

Okay! Hopefully, I have your attention. It should be quite obvious from the title of this book that we are going to discuss a very interesting subject: YOU.

I mean, let's be real. The reason you picked the book up to look at it is because you saw a title that piqued your curiosity, and now you wanted to see what it really meant.

You didn't really believe it, but you figured, "Let's see what this is all about."

NOW HOLD ON A MINUTE! I, more than anyone you know, realize that you, like me, are just an ordinary, everyday person. The world doesn't know us. We just blend in right now with our life and society as a whole. We spend our days just getting by. But what you don't realize is that that is not true. It is anything but true.

Someone once said to me "You are nobody." I replied, "Thank you, you are right and from everything I have read and everything I have been told and taught "nobody" is perfect. Therefore I am perfect.

Hah! But we both know we are not perfect. But I liked the retort.

We all have flaws and our own insecurities, but what you may not realize is that *YOU* can and do change people's lives on a daily basis. That *YOU* were born with greatness and can achieve that status simply by being who you are. *YOU*. By being no more than the person you are on a daily basis. Allow me prove it to you.

I must admit that some of what I believe in and have written about is extremely controversial and will ruffle the feathers of the so-called "establishment." But my sole purpose for writing this is to give you a different way of looking at and seeing yourself, your life and how you fit into this magnificent Universe we live in.

A question if I may? Have you read any self-help books? You know, those books that are going to tell you how to think positive and achieve fame and fortune, sometimes even overnight. How many have you read?

Let me tell you I have read a BUNCH. From Claude Bristol's, The Magic of Believing written in the 1930's to Napoleon Hill's, Think and Grow Rich, to Norman Vincent Peale's, The Power of Positive Thinking, Dr. Wayne Dyer's Real Magic, Dr. Joseph Murphy's, The Power of Your Subconscious Mind, Russell Conwell's, Acres of Diamonds, Michael Korda's, Power, Neil Donald Walsh's Conversations With God and on and on. Some of these authors and books you may have heard of, many you probably have not because they were before your time, so to speak.

You will find this one is unlike anything you may have read because you don't have to do any more than what you are already doing in your everyday life. You really don't have to change a thing if you don't want to. Keep right on doing what you're doing.

But what will change—**AND THIS IS A PROMISE**—is how you see yourself. You will look at yourself differently. You will feel better about yourself. You will walk taller. You will understand more, and you will LIKE yourself. You will be PROUD of yourself. That's why this book is different from all the others.

But you know what? There is no Magic Wand. There is no great mysterious secret. It all comes down to YOU.

It's HOW you THINK of yourself. It's WHAT you THINK of yourself. It's WHAT you WANT for yourself. Is there buried potential within you that is untapped? Do you have the abilities for greatness? Would you be surprised to find out that you do? Do you WANT to find out about THE *MIRACLE* THAT IS YOU?

Jeffrey J. Halperin

We are so busy in our everyday world just trying to get by and survive that we don't take the time to sit down and really THINK about what we WANT for ourselves, or even about ourselves.

Other than to say, that we WANT to be rich and famous. Or maybe just rich. Or maybe just famous.

Have you ever sat down and thanked your Creator for being you? *I use the word "Creator" not to offend anyone, yet at the same time to include everyone. Whether you believe in God, Allah, Mohammed, Buddha, Jesus or some other Deity, you are a child of a "Creator." So be it.*

We are really not taught how to THINK and plan our days, our lives or our future. We have no direction. We don't know how to go about getting what it is we WANT out of and from, this PRECIOUS LIFE we were given. We don't even look upon this Life as PRECIOUS. Oh yeah, we value it. We don't want to die. But do we get up every day and give thanks for the life we have? Do we really believe and understand how SPECIAL and UNIQUE we as individuals really are? Do we really understand how really PRECIOUS our life is and what we can do with it?

Let me stop here. I have broken this book down into chapters that I believe will allow you to follow and understand what I am trying to make you aware of and hopefully will allow you to find THE MIRACLE THAT IS YOU.

SPECIAL ACKNOWLEDGMENTS

If I had to acknowledge all the people who were responsible or assisted me in writing this book I would have to mention every person I have ever met in my lifetime. Some of those people are named in this book, but, of course, most are not. Each one of them, though, had an effect on my life and is responsible for where I am today. But there are some that deserve mention because they helped me produce this book:

My wife Ellie, whose devotion to my writing and me has been a lifeline.
My brother Keith who was instrumental with his understanding of and beliefs in the Universe.
My sister Gail who has always been an inspiration for me.
My editor Calvin Snyder,
My graphics designer and web designer Scott Cleary,
My grandchildren, Vaughn, Cole, Jaclyn and Juliana, who are the reason this book was written. It is my legacy to them.

Jeffrey J. Halperin

CHAPTER ONE

WHAT TO EXPECT FROM THIS BOOK

One of the things that I found in other self-help books that threw me off guard and always seemed to deter me from the path that I WANTED to be on was the word UTOPIA.

In a world with no ups and downs, with no tragedies, with no digressions one could achieve what one WANTED without distractions. Well, we don't live in that type of world.

The world we live in, it seems, will usually in some way throw you a curve. It will very often upset your "apple cart" or create an obstacle and force you to make decisions for which you have no experience to draw from to ascertain what the right decision is. You will probably come to find in most cases that the advice you get from family and friends, while well meaning, is usually wrong.

Their advice will often be wrong for two reasons: they usually don't have the experience to draw from to know what is right for you; and more than likely, they have a different picture of what is right for you based upon their perception of life, which, of course, is not yours.

You will find in this life with the people you encounter PERCEPTION is everything. Perception is reality. Your perception is *YOUR REALITY*. How one views a person or situation is their reality, true or not. So don't expect a whole lot of help from them. And whatever help or assistance you do get, always be overly appreciative and gracious when receiving it. This is not a slap at parents, but let's face it. What they want for you and your life very well may not be what you want for it, and it wouldn't be the first time this has happened.

To find the answers to your questions, seek out an individual who has already achieved what you WANT to do, and even then be cautious. If it happens to be your parent, well, that is just great.

There are people in this world that WILL WANT to help you. You just need to find them. They are all around you, and with a modicum of experience you will be able to recognize who they are. I am not saying that they will tell you exactly what you need to know or take you by the hand and lead you. But you will find people who know other people or can teach you how to get to the next step or level of where you want to go.

Trust me, I waited all my life to find that one person who would see my potential and take me by the hand and bring me to the promised land. He/she doesn't exist. You always reach a point where you have to step out on your own. Then you meet the next person who will point the way. I had so many people in my life I depended on and thought was *that person,* **but** I never went anywhere until I learned what *I* needed to do.

The most important lesson you will learn from this is that you will start to develop your own intuition, your own gut feeling as to what is right for you. And it escalates from there.

You will learn as you progress along your path that you will begin to *draw to you* the people you need to meet to succeed at what you WANT for your life. Strangely enough, that is the way our Universe works. As long as you are willing to put forth the effort, the Universe will help. I intend to point out several examples of this as we go along.

You will begin to recognize the opportunities that you must take advantage of, and with that will come confidence. When you stop and reflect on those events that occur, you will see and understand what has just happened. That will bring an involuntary and reactive smile to your face. That smile will come from within and bring with it a knowing that you are on the right track. It is probably one of the greatest feelings you will ever experience.

These can be at first the infrequent moments that will keep your confidence up and help you stay aware and be able to deal with the uncertainties and distractions of everyday life. These are the moments that keep you going. These are the moments you need to draw strength from when you falter or misstep and begin to lose faith. But be patient. Remember your time frame and that of the Universe may be, and usually is, different. Persevere; don't give up and don't quit.

As I said, these moments at first may be infrequent. You may not even recognize them 'til months, as in my case even years, later when in retrospect you look back and examine what has transpired. **ALSO REMEMBER IT IS NEVER TOO LATE.** I keep thinking that Colonel Sanders started Kentucky Fried Chicken when he was 65 years old. Now, I'm not telling you that you have to wait until you're 65, I'm just saying be patient and be aware.

This is why I recommend that you take AT LEAST twenty minutes each day and sit down in a quiet place where you can't be interrupted by anyone or anything (like the phone) and reflect on how fortunate you are to be you. Sounds a bit crazy, but there is a purpose to it. You will be giving yourself much needed time to think about the most important person in your life: YOU.

I know many people, especially mothers, will say, "My child is the most important thing in my life." I understand that. But if you are not functioning the way you are supposed to, then you cannot give to your child what you want to or what they need. Therefore, you are the Hub of that child's life, and you are the most important person and must do what you can for yourself so that you can be there for your child and for yourself. You see, if you're not there, then there is no life for that child.

Start to practice taking about twenty minutes each day. You can make it thirty or longer or even less. Take whatever time you need; nothing is carved in stone here. Just do it; and as you do, go over the days or even the week's events. Pick out the things you have to be thankful for. You will begin to see how events and chance meetings or circumstances start to connect, and you will also start to see the purpose behind each. You will start to see why some things happen. You might even see opportunities that were missed and some that might still be available. Don't fret over the ones you missed. This is the education part that will teach you to recognize those opportunities when they come around the next time. And they will. This is a learning experience. As I will say many times throughout this book, "It is the education you can't buy but you pay for it anyway" It is Life experience. As all this starts to come together for you, you will come to learn one of the basic truths of our Universe.

"THERE IS NO SUCH THING AS COINCIDENCE."

As soon as you see this to be true, you will understand how things happen, and you will feel more confident in where you are going and what you are doing. You will realize that the "Why They Happen" is because you willed it. You wanted it. Good or bad. As you see these events unfold for you, you will be more patient; and I promise, you will be a happier person.

I don't want to make this seem like the "Twilight Zone," so let me give you a small example of what I'm talking about.

While I was selling life insurance (one of my many careers), I was sitting at a light trying to make a decision of whether I should turn left and check my post office box which I knew was empty 99% of the time or go straight and head for home to make some prospecting calls. In order to procrastinate making the dreaded calls, I turned left to check the PO Box. After again finding nothing there, as I exited the post office, I met an acquaintance from my previous career as a pawnbroker (another of my many careers) and we got to talking. He told me he was considering buying some life insurance for his wife and two kids. We set an appointment for two days later, and I closed the deal.

Coincidence? I don't believe in it, because if I go straight we don't ever meet and I lose out on the sale. Luck? You make your own luck by being in the right place at the right time and it was MY CHOICE that brought me that sale. It was an action I took. This is just one small example of what I mean about drawing to you the people you need to meet to succeed at what you are trying to achieve. There will be others throughout the book.

One more thing on the subject of COINCIDENCE; I have written a couple of novels and, of course, the one thing you dream about as a novelist is that someone somehow will pick up your novel, read it, love it, and decide to make a movie or a TV series from it. Then you have an opportunity for some big bucks. Well, that is still my dream. However, there was a time after the novel was published when I met someone at work who said he knew this popular screenwriter and author and he had a couple of successful movies under his belt. He said that he would make sure that he got a copy of my book. Well I was walking tall after that day, dreaming of all the possibilities and who I wanted to play the characters in my book: Robert DeNiro, James Coburn, you know and like that. Well, Elmore Leonard never did get a copy of my book. And that's okay because it showed me that there are everyday people out there who do know influential people or people who know people in positions that can help me. It showed me that I will meet and draw these people to me and that it is possible that the right one will come along and my dream can and will be realized. It gave me HOPE.

Now, as it turns out, my wife knew an actor who went to her high school who she supposedly kissed one time at some party or something like that. Anyhow she sent the book to him and he gave us the name of a lady who reads manuscripts for some big producers. Well, as of this writing this is still a work in progress. The point again is:

THERE IS NO SUCH THING AS COINCIDENCE

Please remember this. If you keep your dreams and WANTS in your mind and don't lose sight of them, you will draw to you the people you need to meet to succeed at what it is you WANT from this life. It may take time, and that is okay. Just be aware, be patient and watch it all unfold. Watch your MIRACLE unfold for you.

Now I would be remiss if I didn't give an example of the bad, too. I contracted adult onset diabetes after turning 50 years old. Did I want it? No, of course not. Did I will it? I have to admit in a way I did because I didn't take care of my health as I lived my life. I didn't do the things I needed and knew to do to protect my health. So, yes, I unconsciously willed it. Subconsciously, but it was my decision. There is a price you pay for everything in this life, and the Universe will exact that price over time. This again is when Free Will comes in and the choice being yours as to how you take care of yourself NOW. Not later or tomorrow but at this exact moment.

I will give you what you need to know and what you need to do to achieve what you REALLY, REALLY WANT from this PRECIOUS LIFE you have been given. The doing is up to you.

Now there will be some surprises here. You may discover that what you THINK you WANT and what you end up with is totally different. But you will eventually find that it is not. I am the living example of that.

Maybe now is a good time to tell you a little bit about me and what qualifies me to write such a book.

CHAPTER TWO

WHO AM I TO WRITE A BOOK LIKE THIS?

What credentials do I have that would make someone want to listen to me? What credentials do I have that qualifies me to write a book on this subject?

I have what I consider to be a Master's Degree in life experience. Now that doesn't mean I have experienced everything one can experience in life, but it means that I have experienced enough "to get the education you can't buy but you pay for anyway." I have gotten my degree in ups and downs and have seen the good and the bad in this world.

I have seen the saga of rags to riches unfold before me and that of riches to rags. I have experienced the tragedy of an untimely death with both family and friends and known the joys of seeing life unfold. I have seen the good that a person can do and the abuse one can mete out to someone of lesser strength in mind and/or body, how magnanimous an individual can be to another human being and how shortsighted and cruel. Strangely that quality of magnanimity was not necessarily with a person that was financially wealthy. But more times than not it came from someone who willingly shared what little he/she did have.

I have worked since I was 9 years old when I would take my wooden wagon to the A&P food store on Nostrand Avenue in Brooklyn and help people take their groceries to their car or to their home in the apartments behind the store for nickels, dimes, quarters and sometimes a real big tipper would give me a dollar. And when I came home, my father would take a third of what I earned for the household. After that, I got a paper route and bought my first bicycle for fifteen bucks from a kid down the block who had won it in a contest at the paper office. Fortunately, he let me pay him out of my earnings because my father wouldn't lend me the money to get the bike. In fact, my father took a third of my earnings up until the month before my first marriage. Everything I got, including my clothes, my first and subsequent cars I got on my own. I always paid my own way and then some. As much as I resented giving into the household, I have to admit it taught me how to survive. What I should have learned from it I didn't. And that was that I could survive on two-thirds of what I made and should have saved the other third. Shame on me!

The many careers I speak of proved one thing, and that's that I was never one to stay at one thing for very long. I got bored and was always looking to do something different, another challenge. I was always looking for the Gold ring (never mind the proverbial brass ring). I always felt that the Gold ring was just around the corner. Consequently, I have been a Vice President of a brokerage firm on Wall Street at age 28 and president of my own corporation three times. I have over thirty-five years in selling various products, both the tangible and intangible, in the U.S. and abroad. I have sold men's clothing, cemetery plots, life insurance, long term care insurance, health insurance, motivational products, cars, ladies' cosmetics, timeshare property, both on-site and off-site, jewelry on a wholesale and retail basis, Microfilm systems and products, private stock issues, ovenware on a business-to-business basis across the Southeast and Midwestern United States, and cable on both a commercial and a residential basis. I have trained and motivated sales personnel in various industries. I have plaques and awards from various industries as to my success in sales. I have spoken before groups of people, the largest being 2,000 people in Rome, Italy, and, at that time, in Italian no less. (I have since forgotten the language from lack of use.)

More importantly, I have sold for my supper, I have slept in my car because I had no place else to go, I have had everything I owned in the back seat of my car and had no trouble seeing out the rear view mirror. (My kids love that story.) So I have seen the poor side of life but admittedly have been fortunate enough to have never missed a meal. I may have been homeless but never really hungry. I have been in a situation where I have chosen not to eat something because I wanted my wife, who was pregnant at the time, to have it. I have eaten Kentucky Fried Chicken for breakfast, lunch and dinner because it was free, and I didn't have any money. I have eaten Dunkin Donuts for breakfast, lunch and dinner five days a week for a couple of months because I couldn't afford anything else. I may not have eaten healthily, but I ate.

I say "more importantly" because I believe it gave me a perspective and a taste of life, which helps me identify with a large group of people in our country and throughout the world. However, I am fully aware that until you have gone to bed hungry because there was no food and no money to buy food, you really don't know what poverty is. I came as close as I ever want to get or ever intend to get.

I have gone through the pains of a divorce and experienced the humiliation of being a weekend father with no rights. Visitation was limited to the convenience of the mother of my daughter. I learned that being a "deadbeat dad" was selfish and detrimental to the well being of my child and didn't make me feel like much of a man either. So I made sure, once corrected, that never happened again. Even times when I was in between jobs my child support was paid and then some.

My three years between marriages were spent with my daughter. From age 15 months to 4½ years old I was with her every weekend I was allowed. It created a bond between us that will never be broken and was one of the happiest times of my life. She was a blessing that was God-sent. I have written several poems about her and those times. What a joy! I never dated when I was with her. This was precious time with just her, and towards the end of that period it was time with what turned out to be her new brother and new sister. In fact, if I had to work on a Saturday, she went to work with me. We were inseparable then.

To this day I can still picture that sweet beautiful little face standing at the window with tears rolling down her little cheeks calling for her "daddy" as I drove away after dropping her back home at the end of my weekend. It taught me what Unconditional Love was all about.

My second marriage was to set the tone for my life. My wife Ellie and her two children, along with my daughter, when I was allowed to have her, set me on a course to build something I always wanted: a family. I worked hard at trying to get the kids to attach to one another and in building a foundation of love and caring and understanding. And I succeeded.

That **WAS** my **ULTIMATE** goal in life. I remember as a kid of about thirteen when my little brother was born. I was holding him in my arms, and I experienced a feeling that I knew I wanted in my life. That was to have my own family with a wife and children that I could love unconditionally and who would love and respect me. I have that. It is a source of satisfaction, pride and accomplishment that is incomparable. It was good to be me.

You see, I learned a most important lesson in the service back in 1965. I served in the Army and spent my whole military career at Fort Benning, Georgia. I was assigned to Company A ISB, a unit that helped staff the United States Army Infantry School. My platoon had some very intelligent people. One was a chap that I was extremely envious of. He was 6'2" tall, with a beautiful tanned complexion, a great wiry build, could play the guitar, could sing and was extremely handsome. Along with being smart, he had a great sense of humor. I mean this guy was what I would typify as a woman's dream. I saw him one day coming out of the shower and saw he had a bunch of marks and scars on his butt. I asked him what they were from, and he told me that because of oily skin his butt would break out with boils. They would be so bad that he literally could not sit down without discomfort and pain. I walked back into the bay where we lived and jumped up in the air and sat down on my bunk. No pain. I realized that with all the attributes that he had, I wouldn't trade them for his condition. Instead of being envious, I actually felt sorry for him. From that day forward I never wanted to be anyone else. I can't exactly say that I was always satisfied with who I was, but I knew that being someone else was not the answer.

There is a price you pay for everything.

If I have any regret in this life (and I really don't), it is that I didn't wake up to life until I was 50 years old. I was so caught up in searching for that gold ring that I didn't realize that I had what I worked for all my life right under my very nose.

I sat down with myself at that time in my life and went over what I had done, where I had been and what I had seen. It was then that I began to understand what this **PRECIOUS LIFE** we have been given was all about. I learned and understood that I could actually be happy for someone else and their success without feeling envy or jealousy. Without craving what they had. Without berating myself for not accomplishing the financial success I thought I lacked. I saw so many of my friends who were financially wealthy whose lives were in disarray and who were not fulfilled. Who actually were jealous of me and sought what I had and had accomplished.

I began to feel good about myself, and every time I thought about it a sense of pride took hold creating a feeling that erupted from within the core of my being causing a smile to break out on my face that would not go away. That feeling caused my chest to swell from a sense of pride and knowing from within that, "*I DID GOOD.*" No matter what else happened to me, that was an achievement that could never be taken away.

From there I began to write. I have written three novels so far, and two of them have been published. I found that when I sit at the computer and write, I am one with the Universe as I see it. I have no hatred, no ill feelings towards anyone or anything. I have a calmness within me that seems to allow me to love everyone and everything. I have harmony with every living being and, most importantly, with myself. There is a saying that I read in Napoleon Hill's book Think and Grow Rich that refers to understanding the workings of the mind and our Universe. It says, "I know, that I know, that I know." Until now, I always had trouble getting by that second "I know." Not any longer.

Admittedly that feeling of "knowing" is not with me 100 percent of the time. That's where I kept losing it with all those other self-help books. No one ever really explained to me that it was OKAY to lose focus. When I leave the confines of my "village where anything is possible" and have to go back into the daily rigors of making a living and dealing with the everyday circumstances of life, I get caught up the same as everyone else and forget for those moments what this life is really all about. I have trouble maintaining that focus 24/7. I have always had that problem and would continuously beat myself up for it. I would regress to old feelings and prejudices and frustrations of having to cope in our society and the goings on about me. I used to wonder what was wrong with me. Why can't I do it? I'd end up losing faith in me, in the process and in the Universe. Then finally, thank God I began to understand. It's *OKAY*!

I say thank God! Please understand, I am not a born again anything and I mean no disrespect to anyone by saying that. For many years I can't say that I believed in God or in anything. Nor did I even take the time to think about it. But when I finally did sit down and reflected on my life I had to come to some kind of conclusion, some kind of reason or explanation for all this. A Creator seemed the most logical to me and was the easiest to accept.

That is the reason I am writing this book. I found out I was not alone. Perhaps I can help you reach out and find those **PRECIOUS MOMENTS,** that understanding, the strength and the greatness within you. If for just a few minutes each day you too will realize that "**THE MIRACLE IS YOU,**" and you, too, will know that you **CAN** and **DO** make a difference in this world and the life you **CHOOSE** to live. You don't have to be this famous person who reaches thousands or millions of people through the media. But **YOU,** as an everyday person, working an everyday job, with an everyday family (or even single), can make a difference in this world. **YOU DO** make a difference in this world. That difference may be changing the life of one other person, for that one moment in time, who will then change other lives. It's like dropping a pebble in the lake. How far do the ripples reach? You see, whether you realize it or not, **YOU** are a note in the Grand Symphony of Life. Now let's get you started.

CHAPTER THREE

ONE STEP AT A TIME; WHY ARE YOU HERE?

You need to understand who you are, where you came from, and, the hardest of all, why you are here. Then you can decide what it is that you WANT from this life and how to get it.

The most important question to answer is **WHY ARE YOU HERE**? There is a whole host of intriguing answers and theories for that one. And then you throw in Who are you? And where did you come from?

Regardless of what you believe religion wise or what you call your God or the Creator, you are here for a purpose. So I will work on the hardest question first.

YOU ARE HERE; TO LEARN, TO TEACH AND TO LIVE AND ENJOY THIS PRECIOUS LIFE YOU ARE GIVEN.

To learn about yourself and the Universe you live in. To teach others about what you have learned whether that is family friends, co-workers, or people you encounter on a day-to-day basis. Which will result in you changing people's lives if only for just that moment, ergo; affecting the energy of the Universe in a positive manner. To live fully the life you have been given and to enjoy it resulting in you being in Harmony with the Universe and at Peace with yourself. If you will read and learn, I promise, everything else will fall into place.

Now those who are devoutly religious will say that you are simply here to serve the Creator or GOD, "To do the Lord's bidding." Well, you know what? I can agree with that. I might just put a little different spin on it, though.

To me the Supreme Being who created this Universe we live in is God or sometimes I use the word Creator. It depends upon my feeling at the moment and which sounds better to me.

I believe that the Creator wants you to serve His/Her Universe, and that is the reason you were put on this earth. I believe that it is up to you to find out what that purpose is and that is why the Creator gave us "*FREE WILL*": to search out the opportunities available to us in this day and age and find the one that makes us as individuals happy and fulfilled. When you do that, you are productive and you contribute to the well-being of all mankind. You help perpetuate God's Universe to the best of your abilities. In doing so we find harmony and peace within ourselves, which causes us to be one with the Universe and God. In doing so, we find the Unconditional Love for all of mankind within ourselves that is written about in all the books and Bibles and Scriptures from all religions and faiths relating to the Creator.

There is no hate in God's Universe. There is no prejudice, no discrimination, no killing and no pillaging. Not in God's Universe. Those we created. We as Human Beings did that. This is the world we created.

Whenever you encounter a person standing at a pulpit or anywhere else preaching hate or prejudice against any one of God's creations, that person is not speaking for the Creator. That person is speaking only for himself or herself. That person does not represent God. There are no ifs, ands or buts about it. We were given Free Will and are to use that gift to find out what our purpose is while we live our lives.

Please understand that your purpose may be a very simple one. You may be here simply to be the Father or Mother of the first woman President of our country. Or the first black President, or Jewish President, or Hispanic President, etc. You know what I mean. I mean no offense to anyone by omitting any race, religion or creed. There could be a myriad of reasons for your existence and your purpose here. You need to find out what it is. I will help you to try and determine what that is as we talk about creating your own MIRACLES.

Your purpose may be to just be in the right place at the right time to help another person who will then change the world. You may be the person who gave shelter to Joseph and Mary for the birth of Jesus. I realize that's a stretch, but it could be that intricate. Even then you would have to be a magnanimous person who would have had to live that type of life, to be in that position and selflessly recognize the opportunity to help another individual, never knowing until later what you have done.

You could be the teacher of a Martin Luther King who inspired him to achieve greatness. You could be the one who inspired that person to become a teacher. You could have helped the person who inspired the person to become a teacher who inspired Mr. King. Ad infinitum. The links, as I say, could be a chain of events that you are not even aware of but you could have initiated. Let me give you an example of what I mean.

Each morning I get up and make a lunch for my wife to take to work. I give her a big hug and a kiss and tell her I love her and send her off to work. My wife Ellie works as an office manger for a dentist. She leaves for work knowing that she is loved and feeling good about herself and our relationship. She has a pleasant attitude at her job and a smile for everyone. Three patients who come to the office that day are a CEO of a firm of 200 people, a teacher of middle school students and a police officer.

Now, as you know, nobody really looks forward to going to the dentist. But this day because of Ellie's sunny disposition and friendliness these three people have a reasonably pleasant experience. They leave the dentist's office feeling good and with a smile on their face.

The teacher goes to class in a happy frame of mind and presents a positive energy and patience conducive to teaching and handling a bunch of middle school students. They respond to her energy and attitude and have a good day at school and bring that attitude home with them.

The police officer, also in a good frame of mind, gives out three warnings instead of three tickets. One of those warnings is to a woman who was a single mom with two children in day care who would have lost her license had she been given a ticket. She would not have been able to get her kids to day care and would have lost her job.

The CEO went back to his company and actually approved 22 raises because he, too, was in a good mood.

Now is this far-fetched? Whether these stories are true or not doesn't really matter. What matters is that each scenario is possible. What matters, is the extensive effect each of these scenarios can have on the Universe.

Multiply the effect of each person. How many kids in the class will go home with a positive attitude and affect their families and friends because they had a good day? Multiply the effect of those 22 people who got their raises. How many people will they affect? Even the three people who got warnings instead of tickets. How many people will they affect? Where do the ripples end?

I use the simple scenario of a janitor who cleans the public restroom. If that person does his or her job well, the individual who uses that bathroom comes out with a good feeling and goes on his or her way. Contrarily, if you have to use a public bathroom and *let's face it the only time you do is when you have to*, you find it disgustingly filthy. But because at that moment you have no choice, you use it anyway. You come out of there, using your elbow to push open the door, wanting to get home as soon as possible to wash yourself with Brillo and a wire brush to get rid of that nasty feeling that you just contracted some awful disease. Until you do, that has destroyed your attitude, perhaps for the rest of that day.

The person responsible for cleaning that bathroom has affected your attitude and for that moment changed your life. And you don't even know that person. Who knows what the repercussions might be? Who knows how many people you might encounter from then until you get home? How many situations might have been handled differently with different results all because that janitor didn't do his or her job? What will the outcome of those situations be, and how many other people will they affect? How far do the ripples go?

Sound ridiculous? Sit down and give it some thought and think about the last time you were in a dirty public bathroom, if ever. Then think about what transpired afterwards, if you can remember. If you never have, think of the possibilities.

This is what I mean about changing peoples' lives. This is what I mean about your having an effect on peoples' lives. This is what I mean about your having a purpose in this life. It doesn't matter how unimportant or trivial you think your job is. It is important that you do your job to the best of your ability because your job, no matter what it is, affects other people and their lives. Based on the theory of the pebble in the lake, it has an effect on the Universe as a whole. I know you don't see it that way now, but you will by the end of this book.

You see, it doesn't matter how unimportant you might think you are. It doesn't matter how irrelevant you may think your life is to the rest of society. *YOU* are a NOTE in the Grand Symphony of Life. In a symphony, every single note is important. You can't leave one note out or it doesn't work. That is the way it was written. That is the way God created the Universe.

Therefore, BECAUSE YOU ARE, *you are important*. Because you exist, *you are important*. *You are as important* to this world and the Universe as any other person who lives or has lived. Who exists or has existed. Take a moment and dwell on that. This is a significant statement and one you have to recognize and accept. It took me a while to believe until I started to see it work. And it will, I promise you.

Now that we have established your importance as an individual in this Universe and the effect you can have on it, let's see if we can find out what is your inner purpose. The inner purpose is that talent you have that, when you are doing it, you become one with the Universe.

For me, it is writing. When I am writing, I totally block out everything else. All the pain and suffering of the world goes away, and I am in a state of total bliss. I love everyone with no hatred or prejudices. Let me give you a clue as to how simple that inner purpose can be. I describe the inner purpose as that thing which brings you inner peace and in harmony with your Creator.

I have a cousin Paul who I love dearly simply because of who he is as an individual and the type of person he is. He is just a good human being. I asked him one day what he thought was his purpose in life. He described to me the same feeling I get when I write. For him it was simply watching his kids grow: to observe his kids live, grow and become productive members of society and the Universe we live in. To be there for them when they need help and guidance and to impart what he believes is the wisdom he has learned through his years of living. To share in their disappointments and of course, to revel in their achievements. To let them know how proud he is of them and what they have become. And, most important, is to love them unconditionally. To walk into their bedroom at night and watch them as they sleep and know that he helped create this life. To know he nurtured them through to adulthood. To know that if he did nothing else in his life, he did that; and in his mind he did it well. That for him was a worthwhile purpose. That was his elixir of life and his Utopia. That is what he believed was HIS purpose in this life. One child is an artist, one is already a teacher and another is going to school to become a teacher. Who knows what those offspring will achieve and how many lives they will touch and affect. The possibilities are endless.

What a worthwhile but simple purpose. It can be that simple and yet it can be a dormant talent. My yen for writing didn't become a driving force until I was over 50. I didn't really learn and understand about the Universe until then.

Your talent or purpose is within you. It gives you that ultimate satisfaction. It is a feeling that comes from within. When you are aware of it, it creates a smile on your face that starts from inside you and forces its way onto your face. Literally, it does. I promise you it is a feeling you will know when you experience it.

There is a lady that I work with named Becky who discovered her purpose in this life to be saving and caring for stray cats and dogs. As an animal lover, she will scour the streets to find those animals that need a home. At this writing she has seven cats and three dogs. It may not seem like a lot, but there are many she has given away to those who are looking for a pet. More important is the feeling of satisfaction she gets that emanates from within her being when she has saved one of these animals from sure death as they tried to survive on the streets of the city. She firmly believes that this is her purpose and described to me the feeling that she gets when she has successfully done so. This is what I am speaking of when I say that you will know when you have found your purpose.

Rich and famous does not define or guarantee success. Too many rich and famous people are unhappy, miserable and unfulfilled. You read about them in the papers and see them on TV, and they are anything but happy. Don't ever compare them with the true meaning of SUCCESS. Don't be deluded by the trappings of financial fortune. *Understand, please, that I am not saying that having money is wrong or bad. I just don't believe that it defines success.*

It is the reason athletes find it so difficult to retire. They are one with their Universe when they are on the field of battle, regardless of what the arena is. That is their Utopia, and they don't want to let it go. In comparison, few of us ever get to know the euphoria they experience in that setting. Their careers, however, are short-lived, and their biggest battles with life begin when they retire. That is why you see so many of them hanging on to their careers beyond the time when they know they should retire. It can be a very scary

world out there. The adulation, excitement and success they may have had as an athlete is gone. They now need to find their place in society, and in the majority of cases they are not prepared for that.

In one small sense I can identify with that feeling. I had to close a business I had because the industry had changed and chain stores had moved into the area, which I could not compete with as a "Mom and Pop" operation. The prospect of finding a new career or a job at 55 years old was scary. I, too, held onto a business too long that was going down hill.

However, having the knowledge that I have now, I was able to establish myself in the insurance business and found a situation within that industry that fulfilled my needs. It wasn't easy for me, but with what I believe was the assistance provided by the Universe and with the faith I had in It and myself, it was manifested.

That oneness and harmony I speak of is attainable by anyone when you have found what your own purpose is. It is that feeling of contentment, that warmth, that inner glow, that will let you know that you have found **YOUR** purpose. **I PROMISE YOU.**

If I were asked what the definition of SUCCESS is, I would say it is *recognizing what your true purpose in this life is, touching the lives of others in a positive way and finding peace within yourself and harmony with the Universe we live in.*

Whether it is playing a sport, performing a job, a religious calling, singing or playing music, writing, being a parent, being a healer, a doctor, a lawyer, joining the Peace Corps, a soldier, being an entrepreneur. You name it. It is whatever you believe it to be. Whatever brings you that feeling, that knowing that comes from within. You don't have to do it for anyone else but you. It is the moment when you are doing it that the feeling comes, and you know, that you know, that you know. And most importantly; being satisfied with who **YOU** are, being at peace with who **YOU** are and in harmony with the Universe. Life is a "Journey"; the "Destination" is being at peace with yourself and in harmony with the Universe. You will know when you have found it. I promise you. So says Papa J.

Until you do find it, keep changing people's lives and playing your **NOTE.**

CHAPTER FOUR

WHERE DID YOU COME FROM, WHO ARE YOU?

There are many theories as to how our Universe works some are considered blasphemous by those who are of the religious sect so I will state what is uncontrovertibly true.

You have been made from a male sperm and a female egg. However, that feat is accomplished through the mating of the two parties or today it's possible through invitro fertilization. Regardless, it takes a microscopic sperm to connect with a microscopic egg and in most cases to be carried by a woman in her womb from which a fetus will evolve which eventually will grow into what is a human being. Now we have found some very inventive ways to assist this process with cloning and all, but we have never been able to duplicate the process without those two naturally produced human elements.

It is also a fact that we do not know how to duplicate the intelligence, nor do we know how it works, that actually creates the human being from those two organisms. Nor do we know how it is possible to plant a seed in the ground, water it and allow it to get the sun and whatever other nutrients it needs that allows it to grow into an oak tree, a rose bush, an orange tree, an orchid, ad infinitum.

The fact that a human being is comprised of billions of cells, each of which has its own intelligence and performs its own function, has its own life span and in some cases that life span depends upon how we treat it and all this goes on without a conscious direction from us to do so. The fact is our bodies reproduce those cells on a regular basis to replace those that die off, and we do not give one moment of thought or direction for it to do so.

The fact is that as I sit here and type out this message, my body continues to breathe in oxygen which is absorbed by the cells and distributed throughout my system while at the same time it is digesting the pancakes I had for breakfast and distributing whatever nutrients I have ingested from that breakfast to the various parts of my body that need them and throwing off the things I don't need and sending them to the waste collection area where I will eventually get rid of them. And I have not told it to do anything of the sort. My mind is concentrating on my writing and directing my fingers over the keys of my computer. I mean, **COME ON**. Don't you see the **MIRACLE** in that? You do it everyday yourself.

Your brain is the fastest computer ever created and has not been duplicated. We have done some marvelous things in the last 20 years with computers, but believe it or not none of it compares with your brain. With all the technology, we have we have never been able to duplicate any part of the human body. We have developed some parts that can partially replace some of the parts, such as limbs and even an artificial heart, which can help, but that does not even come close to duplication. Why is that? We (I mean the scientists) understand most of the human body and what organs are responsible for what functions, but we cannot duplicate them.

There are so many intricate parts that make up **YOU,** the human being, along with the chemicals of our system that are responsible for the emotions, the digestion of food and the processing and distribution of that food throughout our bodies. The ability a human has to reason between good and evil, love and hate, right from wrong. The ability we have to learn and reason at the same time. The stuff we can fit into our brain is unlimited, and it is said that we use only 10 percent of its capacity. How can you not admit that *you are a MIRACLE.*

Webster's New Collegiate Dictionary defines a MIRACLE as "An extremely outstanding or unusual event, thing or accomplishment."

They also say something about Divine Intervention. Well, I would think that the human body and human being, that being YOU, qualifies on all counts.

For sure you are an outstanding accomplishment of creation. And I would venture to say that the Creator definitely had something to do with it. Whatever name you want to put to the Creator is your choice.

I mean we haven't even touched on our Universal system and the fact that the Earth we are living on is rotating on its axis at a speed of 18 miles per second and we don't feel a thing. Take a look at the moon some night and realize the distance it is from us and yet we can see it and the stars that shine for us are how many light years away?

This whole system of Nature and the balance of it: Why does it rain? What makes it cold? What makes it hot? Some of these we have answers for as to how it happens, but, we REALLY don't know WHY it happens.

Haven't you ever sat down and thought about this? I mean really thought about how amazing this whole process is? And you as a human being are the most intricate and the most amazing creation of all. Therefore, you are forced to admit that *YOU* as a human being are a walking, talking example of a *MIRACLE*.

Another definition of a MIRACLE IS A CREATION THAT RUNS OUT OF ANSWERS TO THE QUESTIONS WHY OR HOW? For example, HOW does the system of our bodies work the way it does, and WHY does it work that way? HOW does our solar system work, and WHY does it work the way it does? Eventually even the scientists are going to run out of answers to the WHY. Thus the MIRACLE of CREATION.

Now I am aware of the "Big Bang" theory and the belief that all this evolved from a single cell. No offense to anyone, but as intricate and as complicated as the system we live in is, I just find it very difficult to believe that it all just evolved from a single cell. I can't believe that it just happened. It just doesn't work for me. My first question would be, "Where did the single cell come from?"

It's one thing to try to get me to believe that man evolved from a single cell. It's quite another when you throw in the animal life, the plant life, the insects, the fish, the birds, and the balance of it all. I really have a problem there. And there are probably species at the bottom of the oceans that we don't even know about yet.

I realize the creation theory is still a stretch of our imagination, and the theories on that are endless. I just find it a whole lot easier to deal with. That being said I will continue.

If we accept the fact, based upon the balance of nature and our Universe, that everything living has a purpose for being here, then so must you. Therefore, there is a reason for your existence, and it is your job as you live your life to find out what that purpose is. That is why you are here. You will decide who you are and what your purpose is. There is no other explanation. If you've got one, please e-mail me.

Now that we have established that you are a MIRACLE, let's see if we can convince you that you perform miracles every day and you don't even realize it. Imagine what you could do if you were aware of the power you as an individual have over yourself and the people you encounter.

One of my definitions of a MIRACLE is an event or happening that is life-changing. I believe that you can trace back through your mind to the moment that change took place and why it took place.

I give examples throughout the book of life-changing experiences, instances where my life was changed and where I have changed others or I have seen another's life changed by something that occurred. Obviously the most satisfying is when I can effect a change in someone else's life by something I did, or more often by what I have said. There is a saying I believe in, and I don't remember where I heard it or read it, but I have found it to be quite profound and very true.

A person will probably not remember what you said to them, and chances are they will not remember what you did for them, but they will forever remember how you made them feel.

When you have the opportunity to compliment someone do it. Regardless of whether that person likes you or not, you have just made them feel good.

In a Dale Carnegie course I took several years ago, I was taught that you can always find something good to say about someone. I don't care if it is the filthiest most repulsive person you ever met. You can still say, "You have a nice smile." You can find something nice to say about everyone. Do it! And do it with sincerity. If you can't do it with sincerity, than hold back and don't do it at all. The worst thing you can do is give an insincere complement because the individual will pick up on that, and it will be worth nothing. But if you can find it in your heart to do it with sincerity, by all means do it. You will have changed that person's life for that moment. You will have made him feel good about himself and positive about himself, and that energy will be passed on to someone else along the way. It seems small and almost trivial, but it really isn't. You would be surprised how far-reaching your one little compliment can travel.

Let me give you a scenario if I may. I was sitting next to a woman in an airport once while waiting for my plane to take off. She was an advertising sales person for some large advertising company and was flying to meet a client of a rather small and unknown company who distributed a line of food products. She was a rather heavy-set woman who was very nattily dressed. She wore a smart-looking blue suit with a white blouse, and her makeup and hair were done up perfectly. She was an attractive woman except for being a bit overweight; and during our conversation, she admitted that she was nervous because this was her first assignment away from home and it could turn out to be her first large account.

I told her she really had nothing to be concerned about because she knew she could do a good job for them. She was professiona-looking in her dress and appearance; she was so conscientious about doing a good job for them she was actually worrying about it. This company was really very fortunate to have her as their account executive. And that was the attitude she ought to bring with her into the meeting. She smiled at me with a light in her eyes, her shoulders got square and she thanked me ever so much for the compliment.

Now do you think she got the account? Yes, I am going to leave you hanging this one time because it is really irrelevant as to whether she did or didn't. The important thing is that woman felt a whole lot better and a whole lot more confident when she got onto her plane than before she met me. Now how many lives do you think would be changed if she did get it? Never mind from the working force but what about the consumers who would buy the product?

Can you see where our little conversation changed her attitude about herself and her perspective about her role in her job? That is a life- changing experience and by my definition a Miracle.

Heck, you can do that all day long. It doesn't have to be as involved a situation as what I described. It could be a simple compliment like, "Gee that's a nice blouse, or a nice shirt." Or, "I like your hairstyle," or, "You have a nice smile." Do you think your compliment will make them feel good? I do.

The act emits a positive energy that becomes contagious, and who knows where it will lead to and end up? That is just a small example of the Miracles you can perform on an everyday basis. There will be others as we go along. It is so easy, so simple and so overlooked and misunderstood in our society. People just don't *see* it that way. Yet I promise you it does work. So says Papa J.

CHAPTER FIVE

LEARNING; PATIENCE

It is a virtue, yes, but it is also the way of the Universe. The Universe works in its own time frame. That time frame is not the human measure of time. It is NOT days, weeks, months or even years. It is immeasurable.

In my poetry, I speak of moments. Moments can be fleeting, or they can last a lifetime. That is about the best way I know of to describe the Universe's measure of time. To have patience one must have the faith and belief that what you want and what you can achieve in this lifetime will come to pass.

I spoke of a goal I had when I was in my 20's and worked on Wall Street. I had set a goal to become a vice president of the brokerage firm I was working at by the age of 30. Well as I mentioned previously, I achieved that goal at the age of 28, but it wasn't with the firm I was working for; rather it was with the firm I went to after leaving the first. The most fascinating part of the achievement was that I had totally forgotten about the goal and didn't realize that I had achieved what I had set my mind to do until I was over fifty years old. I had just gone about my daily routine of going to work and doing the best job that I could and went on with my life.

In looking back over my life, I realized that it was within the Universe's time frame that this goal was achieved, which happened to also be well within my time frame. Now there are other goals that I have set for myself, which have not yet been achieved, and there are those that have been achieved well after the time frame I had set.

What *I* learned from all this was not to set a time frame and carve it in stone but rather to set the goal and ask for the Universe's help and guidance to achieve the goal. I know a lot of teachers of positive thinking will disagree with me, but let me explain.

I used to set goals, some of which were unrealistic in retrospect, and I set a time frame for those goals to be achieved. When I didn't achieve them, I would consider myself a failure where others succeeded. I would beat myself up for not working even harder. Or for getting a bit lackadaisical, I berated myself unmercifully. This brought me down spirit and attitude wise to where I stopped setting goals altogether.

Then I realized that while I am in control of my destiny, it is with the help of the Creator and the workings of the Universe that will bring to me the people that I need to meet to succeed at what I want to do. Therefore, it is my belief that if I am to work with those forces, I must also work within the time frame of the Creator and the Universe, which is not always in relation to my human time frame.

I also work on the premise that "When the pupil is ready, the teacher will appear, " as written by Napoleon Hill, the author of Think and Grow Rich.

My interpretation of that statement is twofold. One, that when you are ready to understand why you have met this person who has just come into your life and are ready and prepared to take full advantage of the relationship, the meeting will occur. And number two goes back to the proper timing of the meeting, which is based on the Creator's time frame instead of the human time frame.

So now, when I set a goal, I ask God and the Universe to help me achieve whatever it is that I want and to send to me the people I need to meet to achieve that goal. And then I add, obviously the sooner the better.

It is here that you need to have **PATIENCE** and **FAITH** that what you ask for will come to pass. Then you must continue to go on with your life and, as best you know how, prepare yourself for the goal you have set. Be ever aware of the people that you encounter, and trust that what you asked for will manifest itself.

This is also where that 20 minutes a day will help you look at the en-counters that you have had that day and how they may fit into your life and how they relate to the goals you have set for yourself. Or not. This is how you continuously reiterate to your subconscious mind what it is you want. This is how you continuously put that energy of thought out to the Universe for it to work to bring to you the people you need to meet to achieve your goals and desires.

Now let me again take a step back. I preach that you take 20 minutes a day to reflect on yourself, your life and your day. Hey, more times than I can count, I come home from work and the last thing I want to do is sit and think. I want to unwind and not think. *That's okay. Take 20 minutes a week or a month. It's okay.* The whole point of the exercise is to do it. I repeat, nothing is carved in stone as to how often. Please don't feel that if you don't take 20 minutes a day that you will fail. **NOT SO!** I will continue to recommend it because I know that over time it works. But again it is your time frame and the Universe's time frame.

Please don't take this as a downer, but I didn't understand this until I was over fifty years old, and I am still learning. Every time I start to doubt, God shows me another piece of the puzzle. I meet another person or see an article that confirms what I believe to be true or teaches me something that strengthens my convictions.

I have had instances of people who I have worked with for over two years suddenly become unveiled and display a talent that has helped me achieve a goal. Oh, it works all right. I promise you it works. The real beauty of it all is to watch it slowly unfold. Like I say, you have an instance where you meet someone and they have the expertise to assist you or they answer a question that you have been wrestling with for a while, or they introduce you to another person or website which opens up a whole new world for you.

For example, I went to a poetry conference at Disney World in April of 2002. It cost me over $1500, which I did not want to spend. But I had this strong intuition to go. I had the opportunity to go to this conference many times before this but never went. This time was different I really had a strong urge to go. My wife and I spent two nights at one of the Disney hotels, and I read my poetry for the contest they were holding and ended up with nothing but frustration when the contest winners were announced and the prizes were awarded. There was no feedback as to what was wrong with my poem and why I didn't win, so nothing was gained from that.

Nothing except for the fact that at one of the practice readings I met a fellow from Seattle who told me about a company on the Internet called 1stbooks.com. This was a company that would publish your book for a fee. It was considered self-publishing and called print on demand, and it opened up a whole new world for my writing and me. I am convinced that was the reason that I had to go that conference.

Please understand that I had three novels written and had no idea how to get them published. I had tried agents who had rejected my work and publishing firms who wouldn't talk to me unless I had an agent. It was now five years, and I was frustrated. I was working a full-time job and really didn't have the energy nor the time to hit every agent I could find on the web and go through the process and cost. I was also dejected from the callous rejections that I received and being duped by a couple of them for money. So this was a Godsend to me.

Through this company, I received notification of a meeting for a writers' group in my area. I attended the meeting and, as a result, got an education from fellow writers as to other publishers, editors, printers, copywriters, and have not stopped there. I now have two of the novels published as of this moment and a third getting ready for publishing. In fact, I have set up my own company and will publish my own books with the help of a printer I will select.

That one encounter changed my life and got me writing again. It renewed my enthusiasm to do so and reinforced my beliefs. Remember: No one is perfect; everyone gets shaky as to his or her faith now and then. That's why I recommend that 20 minutes a day. Sometimes even if the encounter doesn't turn out the way you want it to, just the fact that it has proven that there are people out there who will help or try to help, who do know people even if those are not the right people for you at that moment, it is evidence that it can happen. It proves the system does work.

That's why I say have **PATIENCE** and it will work for you, too. So says Papa J.

CHAPTER SIX

THE POWER OF THE WORD "WANT"

I capitalize the word WANT because to me it is one of the most powerful words in ours or any other language. It is amazing what happens when people WANT something. All logic and common sense goes out the proverbial window. Obstacles are overcome regardless of circumstances. Even laws are broken in the face of the word WANT. When an individual really, I mean REALLY, WANTS something, or WANTS to do something, nothing or no one stands in the way.

Look, I am nowhere near perfect. I have faults, hypocrisies and life-killing habits. I am a smoker. I have tried to quit and have succeeded for a period of time and have ended up going back to it every time. Why? I can't really tell you. Do I have a death wish? I don't know. Again I return to that self-debasing habit of beating myself up for it constantly and yet I do it. I know it will shorten my life and that it is ruining my health. Hell it HAS ruined my health. I have been doing it since I was 11 years old. I can only say that the reason I haven't quit is because I don't WANT to badly enough. Yet there are people, my wife included, who have quit this and other addictive habits and they have succeeded because they WANTED to.

That same degree of WANT goes into anything else in this life. How many times have you seen or know of a person who went and bought something that they could not really afford and knew that it wasn't in the budget but they did it anyway. And somehow they managed to make the payments necessary because of how much they WANTED that car, or boat, or dress, or toy of some kind, or house or whatever. People have even stolen that thing that they WANTED so much and believed that they just had to have or couldn't live without it.

How many times have you seen or heard of people excelling in business or sports when they had less money or less talent or ability than their competitor or adversary. How many times have you heard the comment, "Well they just WANTED it more than the other person"?

I started a Pawn Shop with $3000 and built it into a business with three locations and a cash flow of $250,000 a year in five years. People told me I was crazy and could never sustain a business where you loan money with that little cash backup. Well, I wanted it and did it and it worked for 11 years until I got pushed out of the business by large chains with a whole lot more resources than I had. Anyhow it was a blast while it lasted. But I guess it was time to move on, and I did. In fact that was when I began to write. So when I look back on that time in my life, it was scary as I went through it, but it was supposed to be. And I can have no regrets. It all turned out well as it was supposed to.

People have performed feats, especially in the arena of sports, that were considered Miracles: the U.S. Olympic Hockey team of 1980, the Miracle Mets of 1969, Ali vs. Foreman in Zaire, Arthur Ashe at Wimbledon, ad infinitum. How about Donald Trump coming back from bankruptcy to become a billionaire? How about the job that Lee Iacocca did bringing Chrysler back from bankruptcy or the job that was done with IBM? This is where we begin to indoctrinate you into believing that not only are you a miracle but that you can perform miracles.

If you can perform miracles, then you can do anything you WANT to do and will have the faith to accomplish it—as long as, you WANT to do it. Now let's examine that for a moment.

As long as, you WANT to do it. I cannot stress this phrase enough to the point of being redundant and constantly repetitive, because it is that important. The moment you don't WANT to do something, you won't. And there will be no miracle.

That means to me, and you can apply this to whatever circumstances you choose, and I will give you some examples, that as long as you are willing to do whatever it takes to accomplish something, or achieve something, you can do it until the point, where you don't WANT to do that one necessary step in the process, and then it doesn't happen.

For example, when I was younger I had WANTED to be a millionaire. I was told that if I save my money religiously and invest it wisely I would attain that goal. I also had to work hard and smart and dedicate myself to my career. Well, I didn't save my money religiously. I spent it and enjoyed spending it. I saved some but very little, and eventually I spent that, too. I kept looking for the job, or career or situation that would allow me to earn more money then I could spend, so I could save some and become a millionaire. It didn't happen. I didn't WANT it badly enough. Had I put just 10 percent of my net pay away methodically every week and never touched it no matter what, and had I invested that in one stock, a stock that I was well aware of at the time with its dividend reinvestment program, I would be a multimillionaire today. We're talking 1966 now. But I didn't. I didn't WANT it badly enough.

But I have a boyhood friend who did. He started his career the same time as I did. John stayed with that one company for 35 years. He progressed in position and salary. And he invested in his company's stock. He is now a multimillionaire. He WANTED it more than I did. Whatever sacrifices he had to make in his life, he made. He followed his plan, his regimen and achieved his goal. Is he happy now? Was he happy throughout his life? I don't know. Only he could answer that. He wasn't any smarter than I was. He didn't have any more ability than I did. He just WANTED it more and dedicated himself to sticking with it. Regardless of his motivation, he did it and I didn't. He is retired now and tells me he is enjoying his retirement.

Am I sorry? Do I regret? No I don't.

If I regret it, it means that I would have done things differently and that would change my life as I know it now. That means I wouldn't have the most important thing in my life, my family. You see, whatever I have done has brought me to this day. I am not a millionaire and don't know that I ever will WANT it badly enough to become one. I am financially okay; don't get me wrong. You have don't have to put on any fundraisers for me. But I have riches you can't buy with money, and when I look back in retrospect, it really was what I always WANTED. I WANTED and have a loving family. A wife and three kids who have a mutual love and respect that I believe transcends financial riches. I now have two grandsons and a beautiful granddaughter, with another one on the way. They bring to me joy beyond description. I wouldn't trade that for any amount of money. In fact, I daresay that my millionaire friend would love to have some grandchildren to go with his money.

But don't get me wrong! I still play the Florida lottery each week. If it happens great; if not, I'm still wealthy and happy. Especially since now I am doing what I was born to do.

Sorry for the digression. Back to WANT and how I believe it connects with faith.

Presently there is a young golfer named Tiger Woods who is totally dominating the golf world and has earned more money in two years than most golfers have earned in their entire career. Why? Not only because he has talent but because he practices unendingly. His work ethic is better than anyone else's. He still WANTS to get better. He has not stopped perfecting what he does, and he is already the best and will probably in time prove to be the best to ever play the sport. He WANTS to practice. He WANTS to become better than he already is. The other golfers have talent. Some hit the ball longer or as far, some putt better, some hit their short irons better. But they don't WANT to put in the time to maintain the practice and conditioning regimen that Tiger does. They may have families, they may like to party, they may be satisfied with second place money and still make a nice paycheck of a couple of hundred thousand dollars. In today's era of golf, if you finish regularly in the top 20, you will make well over a million dollars a season. If that's good enough for you and you're happy with that, then that's just fine. That same scenario can be played out in any endeavor you select. What do you WANT and how badly do you WANT it.

Tiger Woods knows he will win any tournament at any golf course he WANTS to. There are days where someone WANTS it more than he does. Then his regimen of practice and conditioning takes over and then the question is can his competitor equal that on that day? More often than not, they can't. Tiger Woods has faith. In himself, his game, his work ethic, his conditioning and the fact that he knows he WANTED it badly enough to prepare himself. He WANTED it, so he did all those things. Others did not. They didn't WANT it like Tiger did. He doesn't think about losing—only winning. When things are close and coming down to the wire, I am sure he doesn't say, "What if I lose?" but rather, "I know how to win." The day Tiger Woods stops WANTING, barring old age and physical limitations, will be the day someone else, with that WANT, will pass him. We'll have to wait for that.

Apply this to anything else you WANT: your work, your love life, your finances, your life in general. Even Dieting. Do you WANT to lose weight? Then do what you know you have to do. That is, eat right and exercise. The first time you break the regimen you know you are supposed to follow, you have to realize that you don't WANT it badly enough. The first time you skip your exercise regimen for whatever reason you must realize that you don't WANT it badly enough. There is no one time or just this once.

The same is true with drugs, alcohol and smoking. You know what you have to do. The first time you don't WANT to do it you have lost faith, and odds are you will not succeed. Here again a lot of people will disagree with me. As I said before, I am a smoker and a professional quitter. In fact, I have a method to stop smoking that I purchased that I haven't tried or even opened yet. Obviously I don't WANT to badly enough. When I do, I will. Now that's not to say that there won't be problems or physical withdrawals. Is it easy? Hell no! But it really is that simple. You created the situation, and only you can correct it. Your physical body, that miracle that houses your spirit, was created to adjust to whatever you choose to do with it. If you WANT to badly enough, you will go through whatever you have to do to change it. And you are the only one who can make it happen.
If you WANT to you will; and you will have the faith that you can. The day you choose not to will be because you don't WANT to. No excuses. Your "God" has nothing to do with it.

As soon as you say, "I don't WANT to do this," knowing full well that it is a part of what you have to do to achieve whatever goal you want to achieve, then you better take stock and check your faith. That's when people turn and say, "Well, it's in God's hands" or whatever word you use to describe the creator. No, it's not and never was. It is, was and will be, only in your hands. Do you have enough WANT to have faith? There was never a question of whether you could do it. The question, was always, do you WANT it?

This may sound tough and unbending. It is. When it comes to smoking, alcohol abuse and drug abuse, you have to be tough. You cannot yield.

When it comes to people who are drastically overweight, it is tough. You cannot yield. You have to have the mindset that you are going to do this.   I am going to accomplish my goal. And please don't put a time frame on it. I don't care if takes a month, six months, a year, two years. Just have the mindset that you are going to beat whatever your addiction is and continuously work toward it one day at a time, one pound at a time.

I weighed 195 pounds at one time and didn't like myself. I didn't feel too good either, especially being diabetic. I made up my mind that I was going to lose the weight, and I did. I lost 30 pounds, and it took me six months to do it. So far I have maintained that weight give or take two or three pounds for three months, and I will continue to maintain and look probably to lose another ten. I am only 5'8"tall, so 165-167 pound is not a bad weight for me to be at. Now I am not comparing myself to anyone, and I know very well that 30 pounds to many people is nothing. It is not the amount of weight I lost; it is the fact that I was determined to do it and I did. Now if I can find it in myself to apply that same grit and determination to quit smoking, I will be "perfect". The only goal I set was the amount of weight I wanted to lose but not in a time frame. I say that because if you don't happen to make the time frame, I don't want you to get discouraged and give up. As long as you have it in your mind that you are making progress and keep fighting to achieve your goal, you will do it.

I love sports and yet I never really pursued them professionally. I always believed that at 5'9" (I have shrunk an inch with age) I was too short for basketball, too small for football and couldn't see well enough for baseball having to wear glasses since I was six years old. Well today there is a point guard named Earl Boykins playing professional basketball who is 5'5" tall, and I could have easily gone on a weight-training program. At 165 pounds I would have been big enough to play football (we're talking 45 years ago people, not in today's world where linebackers are as big as the lineman in my day), and there have been baseball players who wore glasses. I just didn't WANT it badly enough. There is no reason why if you WANT it badly enough, YOU can't be the exception to the rule.

Now that is one example of faith. I know people apply faith to healing themselves and other people. They pray to their God to have another survive some terrible illness or accident. I believe it still comes down to WANT. Does the person we are trying to heal really WANT to survive? Or did they at some point give up, which is like saying I don't really WANT to make the effort to get well or live. There are examples of both. Sometimes their WANT is so strong that they have drawn others to them to help with the positive energy they themselves are emitting, and together they create such a positive force that they do overcome whatever malady has befallen them. Others don't survive. Usually it is because they have lost the WANT to have faith.

Keep in mind, too, that we have spent years doing things to our bodies, knowing full well that we are slowly destroying them. You just can't turn around one day after years of that and say, "Now that I'm sick, I WANT to live." It may happen, and you may have destroyed it beyond repair. Remember you didn't WANT to when you had the chance, and you knew all along what you were doing. Yet there are cases where miracles have occurred even with those people who had been diagnosed as terminal. I believe it still comes down to the WANT factor of the individual, where that individual doesn't accept the diagnosis and refuses to give up.

I have seen it with a personal friend who has beaten Cancer three times. This last time was after radical surgery, but he refused to let go and as of this writing, he is still alive. He has had a lot of positive energy and support from friends, family and prayer groups across the country. And by God he has made it. How long he will live, I don't know. He is only 68. But whatever time he gets, he will hopefully enjoy and forever appreciate the Miracle of his life. Richard is the one I wrote the friendship poem about at the end of this book. He is definitely an example of how the WANT to live can work (More on Richard later.)

Some things warrant and need more positive energy than others. As you work toward what you WANT, and you know that you are doing everything in your power, that you know how to do, you are generating the positive energy to make it happen. The positive energy you emit will draw to you the people you need to know and meet to achieve the goal you WANT. As you continue on that never-ending track of WANT, you will reach a point where, "You know that you know that you know." You will have faith. And you will succeed at whatever it is you WANT. You will have created the MIRACLE.

Trust Papa J. I promise you it works.

CHAPTER SEVEN

DARE TO DREAM

At this juncture take a moment. Sit down and reflect. Take at least 20 minutes and more if you are so inclined. I say dream, but it's more than that. Picture yourself and your future. At least try. This is where it all begins.

What are your dreams? What would be the perfect life for you? Where do you see yourself next year? Five years from now? Ten years from now?

I must admit I always had trouble doing this. I could never really see into or picture the future. I could never visualize or picture where I would be in the future. Or what I would be doing. I never really knew what I wanted to do. Not specifically.

I believe one of the reasons I had such a problem was that I was trying to focus on the wrong goal. I was trying to see what I would be doing and not what I really wanted. I wanted the family, and it was manifesting right before me. I watched each daughter get married. I watched them both give me grandchildren. The family that I longed for was being created, and I was looking elsewhere.

I can't tell you the joy and pride I have when my grandson calls me "Papa." It doesn't make a difference what he says afterwards. That one word "Papa" coming from his mouth is all it takes. I am so hooked.

Or when my granddaughter puckers her lips and tilts her head upward to give me a kiss. (She is at this time only 2½ years old). She is so cute, and she has also learned to say "Papa." When I realized this, the world changed for me. Just thinking about them as I write this, it brings a smile to my face and warm feeling inside my gut.

So now I ask you, what if you had everything you thought you wanted? *I say that because you will hopefully find out what that is.* What kind of person do you think you would you be? What kind of life would you live?

Right now you can plan your whole week as your life is now. Pretty much anyway. You may not know whether you will go out or stay home on the weekend or what you will be doing every minute, but your life is more or less set out for you.

What if it wasn't? What would you do? What kind of job or profession would you look for? What would you do with each day of the week?

Honestly, I couldn't tell you back then. I can now. I would tell you that I would sleep until I got up (which probably wouldn't be later than 8 to 8:30 a.m.). I would eat breakfast, go work out at the gym, come home and write. Two days a week I would probably play golf. I would take at least one day a week to see my grandkids.

As my grandson got older, I would want to spend a few hours each week and teach him about our Universe and how to find himself and what his purpose is. I would do the same for my granddaughter and any other grandchildren that enter my life. I know I would take an afternoon nap. That would be the crux of my days. I would travel some, and those trips would be educational as much as for pleasure. I would use the places I go to in my writings. I would hope to make public appearances and spread my philosophy to the people who were ready to listen. I might also fit in some stand-up comedy somewhere along the line. I have done that and enjoyed it.

There is no question that I would make time to spend with my precious wife Ellie. She is my soul mate and a most enjoyable reason to be alive. Suddenly it sounds like there will not be enough hours in the week to do what I want to do. Ain't that great! I'll just have to find a way to fit it all in. Wanna bet that I do?

Now the only thing that stops me from living that kind of life is not being able to retire and maintain the standard of living I have now. I could retire now. But I would at this point have to give up some of the financial freedom I have now by earning a paycheck. There will come a time within the next few years when that won't be as important to me as it is now, and I will retire. And I will have the luxury of that life. As I said, I am not rich. But in my span of years, I have learned patience. I have learned that the Universe will bring to me what I need to accomplish the goals I have now set out. It just is not in my time frame but that of the Universe. I will wait "knowing" that it will come. And so, I will continue to write and have faith that what I want will be.

What would you do? Think about it. If you can, picture it. If not, write it down. Write a description of what you want your life to be like: the things you want in it—money, fame, power, love, family, career. Whatever it is that you believe you want. Then fold up the piece of paper and put it in a safe place. Every day take that 20 minutes of "self time" and read that paper out loud to just yourself. Make changes as your desires change, for it is not carved in stone. Add to it, take from it, and modify it. As you grow older, your values change and so will your goals. Don't worry; that's okay. Hey! It is your life and you can be and do what you want with it. Once you put the paper away, don't fret about it. Don't try to concentrate on it. Just go about your life. It is already in your subconscious mind, and your subconscious mind is now working for you and will help you achieve whatever it is you want from this life.

When the paper is tattered and difficult to read, rewrite it. Never throw it away. You may find after a couple of years you have three or four or twenty sheets of paper. Just read the latest one out loud.

You will find it fascinating to silently reread the other papers from when you first wrote them down and see the changes that you have made through time. You will also begin to see what you have achieved over that period of time.

You will draw to you the people you need to meet to accomplish and achieve your goals. Reflect on the occurrences and the people that you meet. See how they fit into your life. See how they can or have become a part of your goals. What part do they play? Connect the dots. Remember there is no such thing as coincidence. You met that person for a reason. That incident occurred for a reason. Determine why. What did you learn from that person or occurrence? Even if this is done in retrospect several days or even years later, that's okay.

You might even take the time to go back in your life and determine how you got to where you are now. What occurred to bring you to this point in your life? Who were the people that helped you get here or guided you here or who did you follow to get here? How did you meet them? Where did you meet them?

It is a journey that will open your eyes and help open your mind to what I am talking about. When you have exhausted the why, how, when, where, and who; when you have connected the people and the incidents (I refer to this exercise as to connecting the dots which I devote a whole chapter to later on) that brought you to where you are today, you are on your way to attaining that which you want from this life.

THE most difficult part of this exercise is admitting to yourself that *You are in life exactly where you want to be.* You brought you here. It was your decisions. It was your thoughts that brought you to this place; this time, this job, this house, wherever you are. You did it; no one else. So if you are down and out or rich and famous, it was your doing. You cannot blame anyone else or point the finger at anyone else. Every time you point a finger, you have three more pointing back at you. You may have followed someone else's bad advice or great advice. The bottom line is, it was your life and you made the decisions that got you here. This realization is hard to swallow and even more difficult to admit to especially if you are at or near the bottom.

I have "been there, done that" and I know. Like I say, I have been homeless. It ain't the bottom, but it is pretty low. And I did this exercise I am telling you to do. I connected the dots and saw where I let myself be misled. I made bad decisions and as always, there was a price to pay. But I never lost my desire for what I wanted from this life. Somehow that always stayed with me and here I am so many years later with all that I really, really wanted and then some. Now it is not every single thing. But it is the big ones, the important ones. Go ahead! Connect the dots. I dare ya.

This most fascinating process will work and you will see it evolve. The great thing is, that if you miss a day here and there, don't worry about that either. It will still work.

The other important facet to this exercise is to be the person you want to be and dream of being *Now!* Not later when you get there, but *Now!* Believe that you have it all now and act that way now. I don't mean go out and purchase a Lamborghini or a million dollar home when you are not making, and don't have, the money to afford such luxuries.

What I mean is start to think like that person now. Start to walk and talk like that person now. When you go to sleep, believe that you are that person now. When you wake the next morning, act like that person would act. Walk with your head high and each day if it is within your time frame to do so or each week or month whichever reflect upon the times that have passed and see who you met and what you did toward accomplishing your goals. It may be a slow process at first, but never get discouraged. Know that the Universe is working on your dreams. Know that they will manifest.

With patience and time and your effort you cannot fail. The Universe will not let you fail.

Just be patient and Dream and then give the Universe time to work its Miracles.

I promise you it works. So says Papa J.

CHAPTER EIGHT

TO SEE OR NOT TO SEE

When I talk about seeing or not seeing it is more than using your eyes. When I talk about *"seeing,"* I mean using your mind and your intuition as well as your eyes. I mean understanding what you see. Feeling what you see. Sensing what you see.

When you see two lovers walking down the street holding hands and kind of swinging them back and forth and smiling as they do, can you see the love they have for one another? Can you sense that love? Can you feel that love and does it bring a smile to your face and give you a warm feeling inside?

When you see a Mother holding and cuddling her baby, can you actually feel the love she has for that child. Can you sense that she just wants to hold and kiss that child forever and never let it go? Does your heart swell just a little? Can you feel and sense the love she has for that child come from within you?

On the other side of the coin, I was at my daughter's house one day and my son-in-law was roughhousing a bit with my grandson, who at the time was 4½ years old. My grandson being about three and a half feet tall and maybe thirty-five pounds was tossed over his father's shoulder. His father is about 5'9" and maybe 175 pounds. As my grandson was playing with him, he scratched my son-in-law. It obviously hurt, and my son-in-law brought him back to his feet and yelled at him for scratching him and said, "That's it; no more. You scratched me. No more playing." My grandson made a move toward him. What he was going to do I don't know. Whether he was going to continue to play or say he was sorry, I really don't know. Anyhow he never got the chance when his father shoved him away with a straight arm to the chest.

What I saw was an angry man and a little boy who made a mistake. When he shoved him, it was a form of rejection and surprise that my grandson didn't understand. But more than that there was a hurt in his eyes. There was an instantaneous moment of rejection and pain from someone he loved unconditionally, which at 4 years old he couldn't comprehend. As he turned and ran into his parent's bedroom, he began to cry. I knew I couldn't say or do anything, so I immediately went out onto the porch to smoke a cigarette and to get out of the room. I hurt for my grandson. Tears came to my eyes, and I ached inside.

I know that my son-in-law loves that little boy with his life. I know he would never maliciously do anything to hurt him. I also know that neither he nor my daughter saw what I saw.

When I came back into the house, my daughter said to me, "Don't worry; he's fine. After a few minutes he got over it, and he's all smiles now." My son-in-law had gone to him as I had headed for the porch. What transpired or was said between the two, I don't know. But sure enough my grandson came out smiling and gave me a big hug and a kiss goodbye as I was leaving to go home. As I hugged him, I told him that I loved him. He looked up at me with that light in his eyes and he smiled and said " I love you too, Papa." I felt somewhat better.

I knew he was and would be okay. But I also know he experienced something that would remain with him a lot longer than anyone else would believe.

Now I was not a perfect parent by any stretch of the imagination. I don't even know whether I would call myself a good parent. I was a caring parent, and I know that I wanted the best for my kids and always hoped they would achieve more for their life than I did for mine. So far they are all on track to do so.

I know I loved them. But I also know that at the time I was a parent raising my children, I did not see what I see now. I did not know what I know now. I wonder as I watch my grandchildren grow up what I missed. What scars did I leave with my kids? What incidents occurred in their lives where I was involved that I could have handled differently knowing what I know now? Obviously I can't and don't intend to beat myself up for it now because I can't go back. It is done. But I do wonder every now and then, "What if"?

While I am always concerned about my grandson, I really don't worry. I watch him manipulate his parents. I get such a kick out of it. And I know they don't always pick up on what he is doing because they, like I was, are so involved in parenting and trying to get other things done, making a living and so forth. He will survive, and he will be fine. I don't fault my daughter or my son-in-law. I am sure now, as I watch him, that my kids did the same thing to me and I never had a clue. It's amazing what you can *see* when you are on the outside looking in. I just can't wait for the time when I can sit down with him and teach him about himself and the power he has within himself. To teach him how to really *see.*

The point of this little story is that you can see pain, sense pain and feel pain, even if it is somebody else's pain when you really start to *see*. You see it all, and it has an effect on you. Regardless of the immediate effect good or bad, it is good because it shows that you not only are alive but you are in tune to the workings of the Universe.

The ability to *see* encompasses more than just watching people. When you look up at the sky on a star-filled night, do you feel a sense of awe? Do you ever wonder how it all really got there? Do you feel a bit small? Are you ever amazed that these stars that you are staring at are thousands and thousands of miles away. Yet you can see them glow in your sky. And what about the moon? How special it is to see a full moon with that halo of moisture that surrounds it. How perfectly round it is. How magnificent. To think man has walked on that moon!

When you walk down a street lined with trees or homes with gardens filled with all types of beautiful flowers, do you ever wonder how they all really, really got there? When you walk down that same street after a hurricane has just passed through and that big oak tree has been ripped from the ground and is now lying on its side or worse yet on top of a home, are you not in awe of the power of Mother Nature? Are you not in awe of how she has seemed to balance out everything in her world? How a tree can grow from just a windblown seed?

It seems like a movie scene to me, and I am now walking into this movie and will become a part of it. As real as it is, it seems unreal. It seems surreal, like somebody made all this up. But then what am I doing here? Sometimes I feel detached. Like I am not really a part of this. But then I know that I am. As I rode by the house with the tree lying on its roof, I felt their pain. I felt their disappointment. Yet I was thankful it wasn't my home, and I prayed for those who were devastated by the power of Mother Nature. I was struck by the sight of debris that was collected and now piled 5 feet high and sometimes higher on the side of the road waiting to be picked up. Always a reminder of what a world we live in.

How can something be so beautiful and then be torn asunder minutes later? How in Florida can we have such a violent thunderstorm, then have the sun appear and an hour later you never knew it rained. But of course you can know by the smell of the grass after a rain and how the flowers seem to sparkle and the birds begin to sing. But then you would have to *see* to know that.

Even with man- made structures: how an empty lot in months can become a skyscraper not only inhabited by living, breathing people but having electricity, air-conditioning, elevators and all kinds of gadgets for our convenience. Where do all these resources come from?

The miracles of television and computers. Where did all this technology come from? Think about the fact that the Empire State Building, once the tallest building in the world, was built decades ago and yet look how far we have advanced technologically in that span of time. I worked with computers when I worked on Wall Street in the early 60's, and that computer system took up a whole floor in a building that was a city block in depth. Today I have more memory and a faster computer on my desk. And they are becoming more powerful and faster every day. Why didn't we have this technology back in the 60's? A rhetorical question for sure.

The point I am trying to make is that it took people with vision to create these miracles. It took people who could *see*. It took people who could see beyond the norm and the three dimensional world that we live and breathe in every day. It took people who exercised the power they had within them and realized and believed that all this could be achieved. It took people who had a dream and made it a reality. Truly, it was not done in a nine-to-five world. It took people who had a passion and found that light within them, people who used the principles I am writing about and drew to them the people they needed to meet and know to help them create and fulfill their dreams and visions. They came to know that they could perform miracles, just as you can because the Miracle *is* you.

CHAPTER NINE

BRING IT ON

Let life come to you. Whatever it has in store for you, start each day with "Okay God, bring it on. Give me your best shot." If you will, dissect what happens or as I have said before, "Stand back and connect the dots." Don't get upset; just learn from it. *See* and learn from every little thing that happens. Be an observer and watch as it unfolds. Man what a trip! I admit I don't find this state of mind every day, but I often do. And it is a fantastic way to live. As you drive to work, watch the other people as they drive. When you get to work and are doing your job, step back and look at the other people around you. You'd be surprised what you really *"See"* when you observe people. What you can learn. Even if the only thing you learn is, what not to do.

It started one New Year's Eve not too long ago. I had experienced a couple of untimely deaths in the family, a few hospital visits to family, disappointing news from family members and a tremendous loss in the stock market. It just seemed that whatever could go wrong that year DID. So rather than make any New Year's resolutions, I walked outside to my backyard Haven one evening, looked up at the sky, and said, "God after the year I just had, I don't intend to make any promises or resolutions this year. Instead I say to you, 'BRING IT ON. Whatever you have in store for me Bring It On, let me have it.' It can't be any worse than this past year." And that has more or less been my philosophy: "Bring it on."

The year wasn't all-bad. I always managed to find the good things that happened to me also. It's the syndrome of the glass being half empty or half full. My glass is always at least half full. I have really always had that type of attitude. Even when Ellie and I were first married I was always of the mindset that " things will work

Jeffrey J. Halperin

out." I didn't know how, but I knew they would. And you know what? They always did.

Financially, things were tight. There were months where we didn't know how we were going to make the next month's bills. Yet it always worked out. I mostly let Ellie do the worrying. There was a period in our lives when it got down to crunch time and we received a check for a settlement of an automobile accident that I had had.

You see, from 1980 to 1985 I had one automobile accident a year. Three times I was sitting at a red light and got rear-ended. Twice people made left turns in front of me and we collided. The first and most damaging was when a lady lost control of her car on a rain-slick road, crossed six lanes of traffic and I hit her broadside. In every case I was judged not at fault. But it got so bad it was impossible to determine, which injuries to my neck and back were caused by which accident.

It didn't help that my chiropractor at that time was double dipping between my automobile insurance and my health insurance, so he was not a creditable witness and was threatened with prosecution and loss of license if he did testify. So I received what the insurance companies call "nuisance value." I knew, too, that no matter what the settlement was, it would in no way compensate me for the degeneration and deterioration of the back and discs that would result 20 years hence. Now that it is 20 years plus hence, I am finding out I was right. It is no consolation, but I am dealing with it.

However, I also have to admit those "nuisance value" settlements always came in a timely manner. Whenever we were at our wits end wondering what we were going to do next month that $3000, $5000 or $8000 check always gave us a breath of fresh air. Of course, that is after the lawyer got his share. I knew even then they could never have compensated me for what I was to go though, never mind what I did go through. Realistically it could have been much worse, so I won't complain.

I mention this to illustrate two things, and you can believe what you want. Number 1: The Universe did provide in my time of need. And Number 2: There is a price you pay for everything. I chose by my actions to be at the place at that time where and when those accidents occurred.

I know in the first case I had just dropped my daughter off at her mother's house. Had I spent just an extra 30 seconds with her instead of dropping her off and leaving, I would have missed that lady losing control of her car. Think about it. No, the accident was not my fault. I know that. But I also know had I given my daughter that extra thirty seconds, it would have never happened to me. Probably someone else would have hit her. But then it might have been more serious for her, too, as she and her daughter who was in the car at the time walked away with only bumps and bruises. So who knows, her life or her daughter's may have been spared by my hitting her instead of someone else? Is it far fetched? I wonder.

It's interesting when you look at an occurrence from that perspective. What would have happened had I waited 30 seconds? Stop and think. That span of time could prevent or cause something to happen which can change your whole life. Was I there to prevent the lady and her daughter from getting killed? And to sacrifice my own well-being some years later? I don't know who the lady was or who her daughter was or what she would grow to be. Of course, I can't go back. It did help me some months later when I got the accident settlement, but who knows what might have or could have been?

You never know what lies ahead. Today I look at things differently. For example, if I find my self running late to work or an appointment I try not to rush my way there when I am driving (Honestly I don't do it *all* the time.) It could be the Universe is telling you to take it easy because there is a potential danger up ahead. I have done that, and when I got on my route to where I was going, I was further delayed because there was an accident which made me later than I was when I started out. But did you ever stop to think that that accident might have been you had you not been delayed initially? I do now because of that 30 seconds. That's why I say, "Bring it on! Whatever you got, God, bring it on!" I will survive it.

CHAPTER TEN

THE TIME FACTOR

Time, as I have mentioned previously, is something that you need to be aware of yet not be afraid of. It can be your ally if you take the right perspective toward it. Like I say, I was 50 years old before I sat down and looked at my life and what I had accomplished as much as what I had not accomplished. I can't really say that I had wasted those years because the life I led and what I had experienced made me what I am today. Good, bad or indifferent those years gave me knowledge. The experiences taught me the lessons, and from that I have become a productive, happy individual experiencing the riches that this life holds for everyone.

I have a sister who at the age of 65 has just begun taking classes on painting. At the class she met several women from all over the country who were in the age bracket of 50 to 70 years of age. These women, including my sister Gail, were working from eight in the morning to sometimes as late as midnight practicing and working at their assigned tasks and loving every minute. Their passion for learning to paint kept them driven, and their enthusiasm for what they were doing kept them tireless. Neither age nor time could deter them from their mission.

I at age 63 can spend 8 to 10 hours a day at my computer (with time off for meals, bathroom breaks and cigarette breaks) and never flinch or tire. Am I sore after spending that much time at the computer? You bet. My back aches, my neck aches, and my eyes are weary; but I don't feel it or realize it until I actually stop. It is just something I love to do. It is my mission. My purpose. And I love it.

Do I regret it took me 50 years to learn what I believe I have been put here to do? In reality, no I don't, because I am doing it and enjoying it. And to regret means that you would want to change something and by changing just one incident in your life you would destroy the sequence that brought you to where you are today. For me, knowing what I know now, I wouldn't even consider it. For yourself maybe you would, but you can't. So you might as well stop moaning over where you are and decide to change yourself or your life right now. Right this very moment. Going forward is the only choice you have, so make the most of it. Or not. It's your choice. Life is a lot like riding a two-wheeled bicycle. You can't stand still or you'll fall over. You can't go backwards. The only way you can go is forward, and to do that you have to work at it by pedaling.

I bring up the incident with my sister to illustrate the "time factor." There is no restriction on what age you can start to enjoy your life. It is not after I reach my goal, or after I graduate college, or after the kids leave the house, or after I retire. It is and always will be NOW!

Now is the time. Now is the moment. Seize it now. It is yours to do with as you want. Why not enjoy it! If you are in a job that you don't like, change it; or at least make the decision and then the effort to change it. Put it in your mind now and ask the Universe for help.

Tell the Universe; "I want to change my job. I don't know what I want or what is available for me, so I ask for your help. Please make available to me an opportunity that will give me the means to support myself (or my family) and allow me to grow as a person in a field that will allow me to progress and better myself financially and at the same time be content and happy with my life."

Write it down and repeat that phrase every night during the 20 minutes you take for yourself and review your day. Then put it out of your mind and let the Universe do its job. By taking that 20 minutes each day, you can review your day and see who you have met and what might be available and possibly pick up on something that you might otherwise have missed. Meanwhile, continue on your present job doing the best job that you can possibly do with the knowledge that what you ask for will manifest in time. Don't be impatient. Instead be confident that it will happen and leave the Universe to work in its time frame, which I mentioned before is not necessarily in our time frame. I promise you it works. It did for me.

I was working for the Travelers Insurance Company selling Long Term Care Insurance when they decided to sell off that division to GE. Well, GE wouldn't allow you to sell for any other company except GE, and about 50 percent of my business was other than Travelers, because their Under-writing was so rigid. GE Underwrote the same way. This wasn't what I wanted or, better yet, wasn't what I believed was best for me. So I walked away. This was August of 2000. I was able to get a temporary position with Cigna enrolling their group members, which lasted until December.

Meanwhile I put in my mind the type of position I wanted, which was a salaried position (so I didn't have to go through the ups and downs of a straight commission job) and one where there was no cold calling for appointments. I still felt the insurance industry was a good industry to be in. In January of 2001 I saw a small ad for a salesman by Blue Cross Blue Shield Health Insurance. But it was by a company called Connextions. Where they came in, I didn't know. I answered it anyway and was eventually hired at a salary I could live with and most importantly with the health insurance benefits I so desperately needed.

It so happens that Connextions was starting up a team that was to maintain the website of Blue Cross and sell health insurance via that website. This meant that the calls would be incoming and that there would be at that time a minimum of cold calling. Actually it wasn't really even cold calling as we responded to people who had already traversed and registered on the website. So there was some interest. I have been there now five years (as of this writing), and it has been a great situation for me. Mind you, not without trials and tribulations as no situation in life is 100 percent perfect, but it has met all my needs.

Now I had asked for this in September of 2000, and it manifested in February of 2001. By Universe standards that is not a long time, but it worked. I promise you it does work. You want to call it luck or coincidence? Go ahead. I call it the Universe working in partnership with me. I call it asking for what you want and being patient enough for the Universe to bring it to you and then recognizing it when it comes. Remember: it took me over fifty years to learn this. I continuously make reference to that because I want to impress upon you the *Time* factor. But you can start now. In fact, when you have an incident where it does happen for you, e-mail me and describe the incident. I would love to know about it. My web address is at the end of this book. Remember: the Universe works in its own time frame. Be patient and it will work for you. So says Papa J.

CHAPTER ELEVEN

CONNECTING THE DOTS

I have mentioned this process before, and it is an important if not vital process to use to find out who you are and what you want to be as well as to find your purpose for being here. Please excuse the following use of clichés, but they will help illustrate my point.

It is said that hindsight is 20/20. Another is that history always repeats itself. Maybe not in the same exact form, but the crux of the incident or matter will reappear some time in the future.

When I speak of "Connecting the dots," it is a means of determining where you were and how you got to "Now." What decisions did you make to bring you down the path you traveled, to bring you to where you are now in your life? Were they good? Were they bad? What prompted you to make those decisions? Are you where you want to be? What would you or could you have done differently? Would you want at this point in your life to change anything, and what would the possible ramifications be, noting that your life would obviously be different if you had? You probably wouldn't have the same girlfriend/boyfriend or wife/husband. Maybe you would be in a different state or country. Take 20 minutes and think about that.

Follow this if you can. It is the Cliff Notes of a period in my life. I contracted mononucleosis at 17 when I was going to college and working at an A&P food store. I had to drop out of college and lost the semester's tuition. Then at the insistence of my father I got a job in Manhattan, which lasted only a week because I got a relapse. So I got a new job at Bache & Co. on Wall Street. That lasted nine years and was where I met and married my first wife. I took a Dale Carnegie course to help boost my self-confidence. Then through a fellow named Bruce Katz, who I knew from Bache & Co., I accepted a position with the firm Cogan, Berlind, Weill (who today is the Sanford Weill CEO of Citicorp) and Leavitt. Bruce later introduced me to a fellow named John (I forget his last name) who introduced me to Glenn W. Turner and his organization, a multilevel company called Koscot.

I left CBWL and went partners with Bruce in Koscot. Koscot gave me the opportunity to go to Italy where I met Stan Siehien. After a year in Italy we came back to New York, and through Stan's contact with Vincent Alexander I moved to Florida with the promise of a job and salary. Turns out there was no salary so I left there as my first wife was now pregnant and got a job through an employment agency selling insurance. There I met Gerald Livson and eventually his wife Ellie (name sound familiar?). After the birth of my daughter Jessica, I ended up in a divorce and Jerry and Ellie eventually got divorced. Ellie and I eventually got married. She had two children, Jeffrey and Janis. We were now a family of five. The girls have since given me four grandchildren who along with my wife Ellie of 29 years are the lights in my life.

Now that little capsulated version, except for the grandchildren part, took about seventeen years of my life. Obviously there are a great many details within that period of time that I have omitted for many reasons, not the least of which is time and space. But by connecting the dots I was able to see where I was and how I got there.

You see, we are all in life exactly where we want to be based on the decisions we made to bring us here. That can be very hard to swallow and accept, especially if one is down and out or without a job or family. Or worse yet, if one is incarcerated or who knows what? But we did it to ourselves.

When I was first told that, I was very upset and frustrated. I could not for one minute accept that. Hell, I didn't want to be broke and homeless. I didn't do that to me. It was all bad luck. I made all those decisions with good intentions and worked my butt off to make whatever I was doing a success. Believe me when I say that I could list the excuses for why I was where I was at and fill up a whole legal pad of lined paper.

It was my decision to quit my job as a V.P. on Wall Street to start my own business. It was my decision to go work in Italy. It was my decision to come to Florida, to go on the road, to get a divorce, to work retail, to go bankrupt, to get married again, to go back into my own business, ad infinitum as the saying goes.

Yes, in each situation there were negative incidents and occurrences, which contributed to the demise and failures of each venture. But when I sat down and connected the dots, I realized that in each of those ventures I let myself be swayed by my ego and the quest for the almighty dollar. I was not thinking clearly and with the correct purpose. I was never totally 100 percent positive about the business ventures at the time but it was in my mind a way to better myself at the time. Therefore, I was bringing negative energy into the venture, which eventually brought to me the occurrences that led to the failure I was so deathly afraid of.

This may sound incredulous, but I believe it to be true, and when I was able to look back on those years with a clear head and with the knowledge that I have now, I saw what my mistakes were. But at the same time it brought me to where I am today and because of that I wouldn't change anything. Now 30 years ago I would have given you a different response. Then I would have loved to go back and change a few things and taken the consequences of whatever those changes would have produced. However, we all know that is not possible.

The most fascinating part of this exercise to me was that, had I not contracted mononucleosis (which laid me up for three months) my whole life would have been different. I wouldn't have quit school to go to work in Manhattan. I would not have met my first wife. Etcetera. So in effect that illness changed the course of my life.

Another very interesting fact emerged from that exercise, and that was how much a part my ego played in my decisions. It actually hampered me. Because of it, I wasn't able to see things clearly. It was always clouding my judgment. You see when you think in terms of the prestige or titles. Or how much is in it for me becomes the primary reason rather than analyzing things from the perspective of how am I going to genuinely and sincerely help other people as well as myself? Or how is this going to help better society or mankind? Even if it is only on a one-by-one type basis, it makes a difference.

Part of my nature has always been the desire to help other people. I have only been successful when that was the primary purpose of my occupation. Interestingly enough that was also when I was happiest and most successful. In the ventures where I failed, it was not. Now you may say, "How Pollyanna; how altruistic and boring." True, it may sound like that, but that was part of the knowledge I gained when I looked back at my successes and failures and connected the dots.

Don't get me wrong. It is great to have an ego, and I have a very strong and large ego. But in order to succeed and find your purpose in the life that has been given to you, you need to know how to control your ego and suppress it at the proper time. Trust me, it is easier said then done. An ego is a very powerful thing and can be a turn-on or turn-off to the opposite sex depending upon how it is used. It is a great part of who we are and our makeup and charisma. Learn that your ego can prevent you from finding your purpose and can cloud your perception as to the reason why you are here if not controlled. Learn that it can be a detriment, and when you find the way to control it, you have taken one giant step to finding peace and harmony within yourself.

The other thing I learned from connecting the dots was that the decisions I made while sometimes were done with a clouded perspective, the practice of making decisions was good. You see, not to make a decision when one is called for is worse than making the wrong one. This is especially true in relationships. How often we hear and read about people who stay in bad relationships for a myriad of reasons. They do it for the kids. They do it until the person graduates law school, medical school, or they find another job. They stay for the sex. These are all the wrong reasons and why our divorce rate is so high.

If you are not happy, then you do not project a positive energy and are affecting those children negatively. They see it, feel it and will take up your attitude. So in reality you are doing more harm than good. You can control only your life. If you can't communicate with the other party in a relationship, find a mediator. Maybe between the three of you, you can work things out. If not, change things. You are hurting everyone and, most importantly, yourself.

If your partner is the one who decides to end a relationship, be thankful. Yes, without a doubt it hurts, but you are really better off. That person actually did you favor because the relationship between the two of you was not going to work. So they let you out of it so you could go on and find the mate that will provide a successful partnership in life. At least that is the way you need to look at it. That also helps to assuage some of the hurt you feel when it happens and makes it easier for you to move on. There is no "one and only" for anyone in this universe. There are many, many people you can meet who will be an ideal partner for you. What sense does it make to stay with one who doesn't want you? That doesn't mean that there is something wrong with you. It means only that the two of you don't bring harmony to one another's lives, so why fight it? Let it go and move on.

A marriage or a relationship with another party can be and should be a beautiful thing. It should bring happiness and contentment to

75

both parties and as a unit should flourish. That's not to say there won't be disagreements or bad times, but with a foundation of communication you can work things out. If you both aren't on the same plane, wanting the same things from this precious life or at least willing to help one another attain each other's goals in life, then you are not harmonious and are destined for problems.

For example, here's a big one: if one eventually wants children and the other doesn't, you have a real problem, and it is my belief that the relationship won't work. Never enter or continue a relationship thinking that you are going to change that individual or their way of thinking. Another biggie is not being sexually compatible. Another is not being able to put up with the demands of a career.

An individual's personality and character traits are too ingrained by the time you get together for them to make such a significant change in a time frame that will be conducive to nurturing a relationship. Been there, done that. They have had at least twenty, twenty-five maybe thirty years being the way they are. It will take them at least half that time again to successfully change their character or personality provided they are even willing to try. Can you wait that long? That is your choice and decision.

You know yourself in most cases you become agitated when someone points out your flaws or criticizes you. It's a natural instinct. I know my first reaction is to put up my guard, to ward off that hurt feeling. Now, being older, more aware and more content with who I am, I will digest what I am criticized for and then decide whether it is warranted. Thirty years ago I wasn't anywhere nearly that tolerant of criticism, especially if it was a loved one who did the criticizing because that hurts the worst.

It is one of the most difficult decisions in life to end a relationship. Most of us don't relish change, and we end up getting comfortable in a relationship. Kind of the "devil you know vs. the devil you don't know." But you have to examine all facets of the relationship. Sit down with a pen and paper and make a large "T" on the paper. On one side write down the good points and where you agree; on the other obviously write the bad points and where you disagree. Now look that over, then wait three days and look at it again. Can you live with the bad points as they are now, knowing they will not change? Do you believe that five, ten years from now you will still be able to live with these differences? Based on your answers, make your decision. I believe you will make the right choice. If you are wrong, you will know soon enough.

It is "okay" to make mistakes. That is how you learn. A very important lesson that can be learned from connecting the dots is where you went wrong with the decisions that you did make. What were the repercussions, if any? What were the positive things that transpired as a result of the decision? It is imperative to look at both sides of that coin to get the perspective you need, to discern what was right and what was wrong and then file away the information for future use.

One of the things you have to do in this exercise is to pat yourself on the back for the good decisions that you did make and also take a bow for the bad ones. Hey, the courage to make a decision is a trait that not everybody has. It means that you took control of your life and took an action, which at the time you thought would improve it. Okay, sometimes it doesn't work out so we move on to the next decision and hopefully we learned something from the last one and can use that knowledge later.

Never, never, put yourself down or beat yourself up for making a decision, regardless of how things turn out. Just be prepared to take the consequences good or bad and work with them. If you find out that it is not working to your liking, change it. Assess the situation, and in a calculating way, plan first and then make the change.

When you do this in the manner described and you make the change, you should take time out and do something for yourself. Reward yourself in some manner. Go out to dinner, take in a movie, buy yourself a gift that's within your means. Feel good about yourself. Pat yourself on the back.

Understand, that you have just made a life-altering decision, and if we consider the ripple effect we spoke of previously, this decision will have an effect on others' lives. If only from the standpoint that you are now a happier person, the energy you emit will be positive and is picked up by others.

I know you never looked at it that way before, but it is true. You will have an effect on the Universe. You will have performed a miracle by having a positive effect on the life of another individual or individuals.

Remember: this is a journey that you are on. The only destination is peace of mind, harmony with the Universe and the happiness it brings you. This is you life. There will be good times and there will be bad times along the way. It is how you handle the bad times and the decisions you make that will tell the tale. The good times are usually easier to handle, so enjoy the journey.

That is why I recommend that you take that 20 minutes and reflect on your life. Watch as it unfolds for you. Understand the workings of the Universe and your role in it. Life will be and can be so much more fulfilling and enjoyable when you do. And if you are a parent, you can watch it through your children as their lives unfold. You can be so much more supportive and contribute so much more to their lives when you have an understanding of your own and why you are here. So says Papa J.

CHAPTER TWELVE

THE BALANCE OF OUR UNIVERSE

Here again I am going off the prescribed path but, as always, with a purpose. This next chapter will also be very controversial, but it is important to point out its relation to the Universe we live in and how it works to substantiate a lot of what I am trying to prove. Whether I accomplish that or not will be decided by you, the reader.

There is a young boy who is 14 years old as of this writing and by all standards is considered a genius. Now I know every generation has its geniuses, but this boy is of today's Universe. He has already graduated from high school and has a scholarship to William & Mary University in Maryland, and he has already had a scholarship set up for him to finish his education at Johns Hopkins University.

As a child his grandmother, who he was very attached to, had a stroke and developed dementia. Troubled by this, he has made it his life's goal to find the reason why brain cells do not reproduce. All other cells do except brain cells. His life's goal is to find a cure for Alzheimer's.

Now you may say that is very commendable, and isn't that nice or some other condescending platitude. But remember: this is a child born into today's Universe. This is an Indigo Child.

The remarkable thing is that this child at the age of 14 has his purpose. He knows why he is here and what his life's work is going to be. I have spoken with his father, and he convinced me that the boy is sane and determined. Now how long will this take? I don't know and neither does he. But let's take a look at some things that just might help him to achieve his goal and explore the realm of his possibilities.

Jeffrey J. Halperin

I just read an article in the <u>Orlando Sentinel</u> today, August 21, 2005, that doctors have taken skin cells from an aborted embryo and used them to reproduce skin on second- and third-degree burn patients. It stated that a patch of skin the size of a postage stamp could reproduce enough skin cells to remedy a hundred burn cases. Believe it, or not. This is not a skin graft. This is utilizing live cells to create other live cells. It eliminates the scarring a graft of skin produces. Regardless of whether our government allows stem cell research or not, this form of research is going on all over the world and will continue to escalate until we can cure all of the diseases that have terrorized our society.

In fact, the news program <u>60 Minutes</u> (January 1, 2006) had a segment where a Dr. DeGrey from Britain proclaimed that with the research he has done and with the research that should be done it is now a possibility that a human being can live well beyond the years we are now projected using DNA and stem cell research

I want to clarify something here. While I am a strong advocate of stem cell research, I am not an advocate of creating and killing fetuses or aborting embryos for the purpose of stem cell research. That is not what I am advocating. I do believe that a woman has the right to choose whether she will bring a child into this Universe or not and that the decision should be made within the prescribed period of time as provided by the law of man. However, I do believe that when it is aborted that the embryo or fetus can be and should be used for a purpose that could benefit all mankind, and that is for stem cell research

Countries other than the United States, India and China primarily, are not handicapped by a medical society that is all about the almighty dollar and politically maintaining the status quo so they can retain their power over society and their lofty standard of living.

The two countries mentioned are way ahead of the U.S. in stem cell research, and it will take the U.S. years to catch up. It is also interesting that these two countries are now leaders in producing mathematicians and engineers. Their students no longer look to come to the U.S. for their education. They are now staying home. This is an important trend in science and technology and one to watch in coming years.

They are not handicapped by what in my opinion is a corrupt organization such as the FDA who has made it illegal to cure diseases and maladies by natural means and herbs. The FDA has proclaimed that the only means to cure a disease is with a drug, and if it is not a drug approved by them, it is illegal. The FDA will not only shut you down, they will militaristically raid your lab, home, business and confiscate all your research so that you cannot refute their claims, and they will put you out of business. They will also threaten you with jail and prosecution if you continue to promote your ideas.

The other countries of the world are not handicapped by a society of religious fanatics who have been so brainwashed and engulfed by fear created by a government whose survival depends upon that fear that they are anti stem cell research.

Now the above paragraphs are based upon what I have read and have heard and, therefore, I classify them as my opinion, which under our glorious Constitution I am entitled to do. I leave it to you to decide whether I am right or wrong.

I believe it. I also believe that there is already a cure for most cancers (check out the advances made in Japan and AHCC) but our medical society and the pharmaceutical companies are so powerful and treating cancer is such a profitable multi-billion dollar business that it is my opinion that these cures have been suppressed, bought out, confiscated and/or ridiculed as ineffective, take your pick. Until such time as these cures can be distributed in a manner that is more profitable for our medical professionals and the pharmaceutical companies than the present way of doing business, we will struggle with the soon-to-be archaic methods that are being used today. Blasphemy you say! Perhaps. We will see.

Consider prior scandals with the auto manufacturers where it was proven in our courts that cars were being built with known defects. And it was known that these defects would cause accidents and deaths and their attitude was that it was cheaper to pay the claims for the deaths than it was to correct the deficiency in the automobile. The above statement takes on a great deal more plausibility in our corporate America. It is called Greed and Power.

You see, I strongly believe that this Universe is so finitely set up and balanced that it has provided a flip side to everything. If there is a disease, then there is a cure. That cure can be found within the human body or the plants and vegetation that are available to us on this planet.

That to me makes sense. It is logical that the cures for all diseases are within the human body or in the plants and vegetation that our Universe has provided. It is up to our scientists to find them. My biggest question is are they looking in the right places?

There are herbalists and doctors who have and are studying this aspect of medicine and have found products that can shrink cancerous tumors and can prevent immune diseases while simultaneously shoring up the immune system. Remedies for arthritis and sinus infections and methods for the prevention of heart disease have been found and tested and are available to all. Strangely enough they are now saying that high cholesterol has little to do with heart disease and more to do with the profits the drug companies can make.

I don't have all the answers. I go into this a bit more deeply in the chapter on "Your Health." I have so many questions that it boggles my mind. But I keep encountering instances that to my mind are logical and make sense if you consider the magnificence of our Universe and the miracles that occur.

The most significant one of course is the miracle of birth. If you truly, truly realize the amazingly intricate process of a human being brought into this world and the development of that embryo as well as the makeup of the human body and the power of our minds, how can you deny the *possibility* that what I say is true.

If you truly, truly sit down and think about the balance of Mother Nature, you know the fact that we breathe the oxygen we need to live, which is given off by plants and we exhale carbon dioxide which is needed by plants to survive and who through a process of photosynthesis create the oxygen we must have. This one process should be enough to convince you that there is a very finite balance in our Universe. Animals and insects all have a purpose and a predator for each species to maintain the balance.

Here are some amazing facts, regarding the balance of our Universe. Did you know:

That the Amazon rain forest produces more than 20 percent of the world's oxygen. Think about that the next time you take a breath.

That 90 percent of the world's ice covers Antarctica. This ice also represents 70 percent of all the fresh water in the world. As strange as it sounds, however, Antarctica is essentially a desert. The average yearly total precipitation is about two inches. Although covered with ice (all but 0.4% of it, i.e.), Antarctica is the driest place on the planet, with an absolute humidity lower than the Gobi desert.

That the Amazon River pushes so much water into the Atlantic Ocean that more than one hundred miles at sea, off the mouth of the river, one can dip fresh water out of the ocean.

Does this seem like something that just happened? Does this seem like something that man created? Or could even conceive of creating? To me, all this along with the creation and makeup of a human being, the sun, the moon and the stars etc., seems more like a plan than a happening.

For that reason I make the statements I have written above. Our world is in a crisis. Not only with terrorism, not only with the greed and corruption and cronyism of our government, but with global warming, disease and the unhealthy lifestyles we have chosen to lead. I read once that the human body that our soul resides in was actually built to last at least two hundred years. We have killed it. Our lifestyle and what we put into our bodies has killed it.

Therefore, I believe that the Universe is providing us with a new breed of human being. Part of that breed is the Indigo Child, one who will easily adjust to and expand upon the technology of our society, change the attitudes and values of our society, and, yes, *"Teach"* those of us here what we need to do to survive in the society we have created.

Will we listen? Now it's your choice.

You have *Free Will* my friend!!!!!!!!!!

So says Papa J.

P.S. My money is on the genius to find the cure.

CHAPTER THIRTEEN

THE CHILDREN

This chapter is a very important one to me.

The Children. The little miracles we bring into this world. The miracle of birth, which goes back to the sperm and the egg meeting and creating this life we are now responsible for. What an awesome task, to be responsible for another human being.

Of course, we go to school for this and learn what to do and how to raise them and how to treat them and what to do for them to make sure that they grow up a healthy productive human being. *DUHHH*!

What school? Our only education for this job is the way our parents raised us. And more often than not, we don't believe they did such a good job. Or let it suffice to say there are things that they did which we swear we will never to do to our kids. Wanna bet?

I am getting into this subject obviously for a reason. I know many people will disagree with my findings and opinion but I believe this has to be screamed out to the masses. So here goes.

The children we are bringing into this world today, and probably for the last fifteen and maybe as much as twenty years, are different from what we were twenty, thirty or forty years ago. They are smarter. They are more spiritual. By that I mean that they are more in tune with the Universe than we ever were or may even be at present. They are more intuitive. They learn faster and become more easily bored. Their imagination is more expansive. Now I am over sixty years old, so when I reflect on my childhood there is a

85

large majority of you who may read this that will never identify with what I am going to say here.

When I was a kid in Brooklyn, we didn't have all the toys and electronic diversions that kids have today. If we as a child were dumped into today's world, we would be totally lost. I never was allowed to stay in the house after school. I was always told to go out and play. I didn't like being sent to my room to play. There was nothing there, so I had to make up stuff to keep myself occupied. I made believe I was the Lone Ranger or Buck Rogers, and I would punch my pillow, which was the bad guy, as I saved the damsel in distress. My sister's pillow was the damsel. Or I would take out my little plastic soldiers and play war. I would take the blanket and stretch it from the chair to the bed and make a fort. Stuff like that. When I went outside, we played stoop ball or stick ball in the street or hand ball against a building or punch ball on the sidewalk. We played iron tag with the fences or the telephone poles. We played hide and seek.

I watch my grandkids now, and they have all these electronic toys and computers that make all kinds of sounds and music. I still can't work most of them. But because they don't know any better, they adjust rapidly and they make do. At three years old my grandson could work a VCR. He knew how to put the tape in and press the proper remote button to make it play. Now he has graduated to the DVD at five. I still have trouble working my DVD player.

The point here is that this is a faster society than when we were kids. The world is at your fingertips with the Internet. Business is done over the computer, and many times you never even get to meet the person you are dealing with. Transactions are completed across continents via the Internet, which couldn't be done when we were kids.

What I am pointing out is that this is a different world and so are the kids that we are now bringing into it. Each generation has it's own purpose and responsibilities to the Universe.

I believe that my generation was responsible for the outbreak of introspectiveness. We started the psychological revolution and psychotherapy. We were the ambitious ones during the fifties and early sixties that quested for the almighty dollar at any cost including the cost of family relationships, which is something we regretted many years later.

The generation that came after mine was responsible for the outbreak of self-gratification or thinking about satisfying oneself and connecting to the Universe. These were the so-called hippies and flower children.

Each generation had a purpose and led us to where we are now. With each generation we became more enlightened about ourselves, and what makes us tick. We became more aware of relationships and the family as a harmonious unit. It was my generation that started the rage of divorce and the next generation carried it even further.

My generation saw the miracle of television come into the home. I remember in 1968 with my first marriage I had to have a 25" television. That was the largest screen at that time, and the best. TV became an important part of our existence. We were ready and ripe for that. Then VCR's came along. Then along came cable. Now we have the Worldwide Internet.

We, my generation, weren't ready for today's world. I think about my father and the decades and changes he had to adapt to. The invention of the automobile was the first. Can you even conceive of being without some sort of vehicle today? Then there was just radio. Heck, we have I-Pods now.

Then he had the Great Depression to deal with and World War II. The evolution of change hit the fifties, and the chaos of the sixties meant the advent of computers. The craziness of the seventies: an inflation rate that was astronomical, economic changes in the eighties and the electronic age of the nineties. There was no way he could adapt to all that change. And, he didn't.

I don't know where I will be 20 years from now or what the world will be like. With all the strides and advancements we have made in just the last 20 years, who knows what the next 20 will bring? Hell, I'm a good ten to fifteen years behind today's world. But I am sure the people of this world and this generation can teach me.

That's the beauty of the system. Our teachers are not only the ones sitting behind the desk in school. They are all over and of all ages, especially the younger generation. Yes, we hope they will learn some of the things that we have experienced and are willing to share with them, but they are also *OUR* teachers. I also hope they exhibit the patience with us that we supposedly did and should have with them.

I attribute this to the makeup of our Universe, which is why I see our whole existence as one enormous miracle. This magnificent Universe prepares you for the world you are being brought into even if you don't realize it or acknowledge it. When you get a chance, sit down and think about that.

Let's face it. It used to be that you grew up in a neighborhood and raised your family in the same neighborhood. You went to the same schools as your parents or older brothers and sisters did. Now we are universal. Because of the way society is, it is the norm for a son or daughter to find a job in another city, state or even country. But there is a truism that still works. "The apple does not fall far from the tree." In the greater majority of cases, you will raise your kids based upon the way your parents raised you.

With today's children it really doesn't work for them. Now I am not against, and I believe wholeheartedly in, family values. To me, the most important thing is family. It was my goal to achieve that, and I have. But I also realize that because of the type of children we are bringing into this world, we must adapt.

It will boggle the mind to find out the statistics on the number of today's children who have been diagnosed with ADD or ADHD and have been prescribed medication such as Ritalin and Adderall and the like.

There is a website called www.indigochild.com If your child has been diagnosed with ADD or ADHD please go there and read about it. The book "the Indigo Children" should be required reading for every parent and every teacher. It is amazing what you will learn about your child.

Part of the problem holding these kids back is that our teachers and doctors and the adults now running our world are from the old schools and have not, I will be kind here and say, totally adapted to the world we live in when it comes to raising our children. Old attitudes and beliefs are hard to give up and shake off. The world has changed, and we are trying to hold on to antiquated theories and mores and values that don't work with today's children in today's society. You will see a drastic change in the next 20 years.

Teachers in our schools are probably the hardest hit as far as having to deal with these children, especially the older teachers. They don't have the education, the patience, or the awareness to deal with the kids coming into their classes. I realize that this may be an unfair generalization, but it is one I very strongly believe based on what I hear and what I see of today's teachers. It's not easy for them, I know; but the higher educational institutions are not prepared and, therefore, can't teach the teachers who are and will be teaching our kids.

I'll bet you that if you asked 20 teachers what is their opinion on, and how do they deal with, an Indigo Child, fifteen won't know what you are talking about.

The doctors in today's society are too quick to solve problems with pills. As soon as they see a child they deem is difficult to handle, they prescribe Ritalin or Adderall or some other psychotic medication, which slows them down both metabolically and also their thought and learning process.

In an article in the <u>Orlando Sentinel</u> during the week of February 6, 2006 it was noted that these drugs (Ritalin and Adderall were specifically named in this study) increase the risk of heart attacks, strokes and sudden death. It also states that a majority of the members of the panel of drug safety experts "concluded the evidence of serious risks was so great that a strong new warning – not just more research – was needed." Dr. Steven Nissen, a Cleveland Clinic cardiologist said, "This is an out-of-control use of drugs that have profound cardiovascular consequences." For children under the age of eighteen the number of strokes was higher than expected but the number of heart attacks was lower.

It did not give specific census data for children and adults, but just that comment alone would cause me to find another way to control my child's behavior. I would exhaust all possibilities before I would put my child on that type of drug.

Here again I know I am making a generalization, but I have just seen too much of it. The parents need to try other methods first and then have the patience that the methods will work. One of the most important as I mentioned before is nutrition. You would be surprised what a difference it makes.

The other is taking the time to sit and actually talk and converse with these kids. While the children don't understand what makes them do the things they do, surprisingly enough they will understand to a great degree if you will take the time to explain it to them. At three years old and up, the Indigo Child will comprehend if you keep it simple and talk to him or her. They have the capacity to do that. If they are smart enough to pick up on your energy and they do and will, they are also smart enough to comprehend why they are reacting the way they do. I strongly believe this. Try it. Then have the patience to allow it to work.

The Indigo Child is very attached to the mother until about seven years old. They will attach to the father too, but let's not forget or in any way underestimate the attachment to the mother who carried them and gave birth to them. These are also very, very loving and affectionate children.

I talk about a parent having patience, and I must mention this. I know that today's society, in the greater majority of households, both parents are required to work. That makes it very difficult and also time constricting to find the time to do this and have the patience necessary with all the other responsibilities that a parent has. In the case of the single parent, it is even more difficult to do so. But don't forget, it was your decision to bring this little miracle into this world. Your primary responsibility has to be to give that child whatever it needs to grow up and be a productive individual. I grant you it is not easy, but it is **your** job. Therefore, you need to find a way to educate yourself as to what those needs are and fulfill them.

This is definitely a case of "Don't do what I did," rather, "Do what I say." I didn't know this when I was a parent of younger children or I would have done so many things differently.

I mention all this to bring you into the meat of what I really want to get to, and I will relate this after I set the scene. Back to the children.

Have you ever walked into a room or gone to a party and as you walked into the room, even though you may have known all the people or some of the people or maybe none of the people, you just felt weird? Like you didn't really belong there? Or you didn't feel comfortable there? Or there was a feeling that you really couldn't put your finger on, but it just didn't seem right for you to be there?

Have you ever met a friend after a long time of not seeing him or her, months maybe years, and you felt like something had changed and you didn't feel the same about that person anymore?

Have you ever met someone for the first time and whether you shook hands or not you just didn't like that person, or feel comfortable with that person, or just got some bad vibes from that person? Like your first impression was not a good one?

This is energy at work. It may be your energy, his or her energy or the energy of the people around you. When you feel something isn't right, it isn't. That is your intuition at work. You project an energy, positive or negative, depending upon your circumstances and the people you are with. It also depends upon what you believe and what your values are.

For example, I have a problem with doctors. I don't trust them, especially when they display this "God-Like" complex where they imply and sometimes even believe that, because he or she is the doctor, you should do what they say and not question it. So when I walk into a doctor's office, I walk in with an attitude. First off I know I am not going to be taken in on time as they are always behind and late. So I know right off I am going to have to wait. Second, more than likely the doctor doesn't even know why I am there. So I give off these negative vibes, and the staff picks up on that so they're not as cordial as I want them to be. Now this is all my fault because this is my negative energy and it transmits to everyone in that office eventually. Therefore, my blood pressure reading is always higher when I walk in than it is when I am about to leave. It's called "white coat syndrome." But it is still my fault.

Basically I am a positive person and will usually emit a positive energy source for others to pick up on. I make sure I always have a kind word or compliment for everyone, subtly not overtly. I am sincere when I do it.

Example: I was shopping with my wife one night, and we were in a woman's clothing store. While she was trying on clothes, I began a conversation with a salesman. After idle chat he told me he was going to college to become a teacher and this was a job to help pay his tuition and get him through school. He said he wanted to teach algebra to first and second year high school students. I commended him on his choice of vocation, as we need good teachers. He also added that he felt he could identify with kids that age and that he wanted to share his life experiences and possibly mentor them in a way that could prevent them from making some of the mistakes that he had encountered in his life. I again commended him and told him "You will be successful, and you will attain the goal you have set." He stared at me and stated quizzically, "How do you know? You don't even know me."

I responded, "I know enough about you. I know that you are willing to take a job like this and do what you have to do to achieve a goal you have set for yourself. That shows a willingness to work hard as a means to an end to achieve a worthwhile goal. For me, that's knowing enough to know that you will succeed." He looked at me, shook my hand, smiled and said "Thank you"

I replied, "You are most welcome and good luck"

A few minutes later my wife and I left the store, and the salesman waved at me as we exited. Now I know that that salesman left the store feeling good about himself. That to me is an example of emitting positive energy and at the same time performing a little miracle with this young man. For that moment his life was changed. Some stranger had just convinced him that he would succeed. I tell you what: I felt good leaving that store knowing what I had done.

Energy is all around you all the time. Every person emits energy from his/her being. You have heard the term "Body Language" used in so many ways and forms. That is connected to the energy you emit and the aura of yourself that you project.

Ever notice how when some people walk into a room all heads turn. Whether it is male or female some people just have that aura about them. Now you have this energy or Aura at home with your kids, too. It may be the loving parent sometimes or the disciplinarian sometimes or the hassled parent who just wants quiet. It may be the fearful parent who is unsure of what to do as a parent or how to handle his or her own life crisis. Or fearful of how to be a parent.

Whatever the aura or energy you project, your children will pick up on it. In many cases they will emulate it. They don't realize they are doing it, and you will never realize it because you are too wrapped up in your moment to notice the subtle changes. In many cases you throw it off to the terrible twos or the threes or they are tired or hungry or a dozen other reasons that have no validity except in your world.

I know my grandson will yell at his parents to stop yelling when they shout at each other in an argument.

Many psychiatrists will tell you that when a couple gets divorced, which is so prevalent in our society today (I did it myself thirty some odd years ago), the children very often believe that it was their fault.

As I said before, these children of today are different. They are more intuitive and more spiritual. It is an innate quality that will manifest and come to fore in later years.

The whole crux of this chapter is that the children will pick up on your fears and insecurities and take these issues as their own. That will be the baggage, the energy, that they carry around with them. That will have an affect on their behavior, their attitude and their health. And you will never know it unless you are aware of it. The next time your child comes down with a cold, examine your own attitude and life at that moment in time. Were you upset, uptight or angry at something or someone? Make a note of it. See if it doesn't coincide with their illness. I believe you will be surprised.

Example: I know someone who is very close to me that has had insecurities about herself and her ability to be a good parent and do the right thing for her child. She has always been insecure about herself because of the type of upbringing she had. Her mother was an extremely insecure person. Her mother would constantly berate her and put her down, sometimes even in front of other people. While she is married to a wonderful man and is a successful businesswoman in her own right, that insecurity grew and festered. This apple did not fall far from that tree.

This insecurity is now being transferred to her child. In this case the mother is not overtly making the child insecure about herself as was done to her, but the child picks up on the mother's angst because of the type of child that she is. She loves her child as life itself but cannot see and doesn't realize her own insecurities and how they are being transferred to her child. She is so afraid of not being the perfect parent or being inadequate. She heaps such guilt on herself if she doesn't spend every possible moment with her child. You see, she is trying to be the mother that she never had and wanted. She also will not believe what I have said here.

This is what I mean about the energy you project to others and what they will pick up on. The mother doesn't realize that she is a good, capable and very loving mother. She doesn't realize that she has all the tools she needs to guide her child through today's world. She just needs to believe it and believe in herself.

You see, perception here is a very important facet of a child's life. They will see a situation differently than we will. That is why many times in a parent/child relationship, years after, an incident will be brought up in a conversation and a parent will look at the child and finally find out what their perception of that incident was and how different it was from their own. There are times where a child's perception of their life will cause estrangement between the child and parent. And the worse part is that the parent has no clue why.

Children today are very resilient and more so than we give them credit for. They in some ways are already smarter than we are; they just don't know it yet.

The point here is you must be aware of the energy you project and what it is you are projecting, especially at home because your child will pick up on it and make it his/her own. When you see variances in your child's behavior, check your own. Check yourself and see if you didn't come home tired or angry or uptight. I assure you, that is what you are projecting to your child regardless of the words that come out of your mouth.

There is a young mother I work with who has a four-year old son named Jordon who was diagnosed with ADHD and put on medication. I related to her exactly what I have written above, and she looked at me and said, "You know, you're right. It's true. When I am uptight and can't sleep, neither does my son. He doesn't sleep either. Now that I stop and think about it, when I am relaxed and not uptight, so is he."

She told me how he got up one Saturday morning and was bored. So she told him that she had to clean the house and then she would find something for them to do. He asked if he could help her clean. She told him that he could if he wanted to. He cleaned his room, did the dishes and dusted the living room and vacuumed it. She was amazed. This is a four year old. "And he did a good job, too," she said.

Explain it to children and reassure them that you are okay and they are okay and that you love them. Tell them that you had a bad day at work or are having trouble making ends meet but that every thing will be okay and try to make yourself believe it, too. Besides, you will actually feel better about whatever is bothering you just by being able to speak of it and get it out of your system. You may also be very surprised at the questions and reaction you may get from your child.

Now here again people will be up in arms about talking to, let's say, a four year old about making ends meet. But I believe it is much more therapeutic to get it out of your system and at the same time allay the fears and concerns a child may have as they pick up your negative energy. The child may not understand what "making ends meet" means, but he or she will most definitely understand that you took the time to talk to him or her and reassure him or her that all will be okay. That, they will believe, which will put them at ease. Give your children some credit for the miracle that they are.

If I may, reiterate and be redundant because of its importance: Before you so quickly let a doctor put your child on a medication and diagnose him/her with ADD or ADHD and mark them for life, see a nutritionist. Let the nutritionist put the child on a diet, one where he or she is eating the right foods. And not all the sugars and white flours and pastas and fast foods and the easy things to cook. Learn about nutrition and how the foods eaten affect your child. I know this isn't easy, but it is something that you need to do as a parent in today's Universe. A byproduct of this is that you will have put your child on a program of eating healthily and taught him/her how to and why they should do this, which will be a practice he/she can follow for his/her entire life. They then can teach their kids, your grandkids. That can't be too bad.

You might also have the doctor test for chemical or hormone imbalances in the child. These too can often cause irregular behavior, especially if it involves the thyroid.

I am doggedly of the belief that a good portion of the children on medication today should not be on it and would be considered "normal" children with the right diet. I also believe that parents, despite their crazy schedules, need to have more patience and understanding of whom they are dealing with and what their needs are. Their needs are different from the ones you had as a child.

You need to determine what they are and then meet them. Surprisingly enough you can compromise with today's children even in their younger years. I am very well aware that this statement will rankle some people to the point of extreme anger. While I apologize for getting you upset, I will not back down on I what I've said. It is true, and I challenge you to check it out. I *know* your child is worth it. Do you?

I could go on and on here because it is such a sensitive and controversial subject. And it is one that is very dear to my heart. Seek out the experts in this field. Your kids are worth it.

I promise you. So says Papa J.

CHAPTER FOURTEEN

THE TEENAGERS

This is for those between the ages of 13 and 19, a group of people who also are a very integral part of our Universe and important to the survival of our World as we know it today.

This age is also the scariest age for a parent. This is about the time when a parent has lost patience, and the conflict between a parent and child reaches a peak of contention. It is where a parent very often loses communication with the adolescent and has difficulty maintaining control of him/her.

It is when the teenager starts to adopt the attitude that his/her parents are not only out of step and out of tune with today's world but that they are an obstacle to their growth as an individual and their chosen lifestyle.

Of all the age groups one can categorize, *YOU,* the teenager are the most volatile, the most rebellious and probably the most likely to initiate change in our society. I say that because of your rebellious nature. It is you, the teenager who will popularize the next generation of Music, TV programs, fashion, hairstyles and artists of all genres. You will take it with you as you grow and become recognized as an adult.

Do you as a teenager recognize the effect you will have on the world you create for yourself and others? Do you realize the responsibility you have to yourself in this matter? You really need to step back and realize the power you have and the effect you will have on the world. I have two words for you, *Patience* and *Caution.* Your turn will come. Start to *SEE* now. Open your eyes and see the world around you. Work to understand it and live within its framework. *For now.* Your opportunity is on the horizon; be patient just a little while longer, and it will be your world. I say be cautious so as not to do anything so radical that you rob yourself of your opportunity.

Example: It was my generation who initiated Rock and Roll, which was the cornerstone of the music industry and the variations that evolved from it. It was my generation that popularized the slicked back hairstyles for men and fashions for women. The movies played to that with Marlon Brando's The Wild One and James Dean's Rebel Without a Cause." The TV programs took a while longer before pandering to my generation, but eventually they came around too. In today's world of television with the addition of cable, society reacts a lot more quickly to trends than before because there are so many more channels to choose from. Well *YOU,* the teenager, will have that same effect. How will you handle it?

You see, you don't realize that you are participating in changing society and the world you live in. You don't yet realize the power you actually have. You are so caught up in your own little world of trying to assert yourself and your independence and battling your parents that you overlook your importance as an individual.

You haven't yet learned that *YOU* are a Miracle. *YOU* have greatness in you. *YOU,* too, are a note in the Grand Symphony of life. You have entered a world, which is ever changing as far as technology goes. You grow up dealing with that technology and learning about the new innovations. You actually are more adept at using them than your parents are. People like myself are so far behind that it is shameful, so you are at least a step ahead of all of us.

Now sit down for a few minutes. I want you to take stock of yourself. You are at an age where you are still soaking up knowledge. You are absorbing at a faster pace than any other generation except for the children behind you who haven't learned what you know yet. This should be a very exciting time of your life and one which will in retrospect go by very fast. You are rushing to become "of age," to become an adult. Don't.

You are at a time in your life where, if anything, you need to slow it down. Take your time. Enjoy these years and by all means learn everything you can about everything you can. *The one constant that will separate you from the masses is knowledge.*

Knowledge is power. You need to gain knowledge of how this Universe we live in works. You need to gain knowledge of what makes you tick. You need to gain knowledge about every subject you come upon. Now is the time. Your brain is like a sponge and will absorb almost everything you expose it to.

This Worldwide Web gives you infinite possibilities to learn about every subject imaginable. Learn, learn and learn until you are exhausted. I promise you, you will thank me at a later date.

You have the opportunity to get things right, right from the start. Learn about nutrition and what and what not to put into that miraculous vessel that houses your Spirit that is called your body. Learn about the herbs and vegetation provided by the Universe that you live in that can help you maintain your health and prevent some of the diseases and health problems that have affected my generation and will eventually affect your parents. Learn it now.

Learn about the history of your country and of society in general. There is a reason for this. If you learn the history of a generation, you have a better chance to understand the people of that generation and what makes them tick and why they think like they do, ergo, your parents.

You are in a state of flux right now as a teenager. Your body is changing and hormones are racing and you are discovering or about to discover sex, as well as yourself. You are finding it difficult in understanding your parents and the reasons behind a lot of the things they require and tell you to do. That is the job and fate of the teenager. This has been going on for centuries.

As the child becomes a teenager and becomes an individual with a certain amount of knowledge, she now wants the privileges of being an adult. Or he wants to be heard and not recognized as a child anymore. The teenager now asserts his/her independence. She wants her privacy. He wants his space. The parents suddenly become an adversary, and the teenager goes off and begins to experiment by making various decisions on his or her own. In many cases the decisions made conflict with the views of the parents. It may be about their dress, their music, their friends, their chores, how they think.

The parents on the other hand forget that they did exactly the same thing as teenagers. But in this society a parent's job in raising their kids is more a matter "Do as I say, not as I do or did." Because the parents have done most or some variation of what their teenagers have done, are going to do, or have thought about doing, they are aware of the pitfalls and dangers too, if I may, and will most often try to prevent their teenagers from doing things like that. They will also have some variation of a punishment waiting for them when and if they do those things.

There is no need for examples or specifics here, for I am positive each parent knows exactly what I am talking about. Every one of us without exception will remember something that they did as a teenager that they would not want their kids to do. But please, parents, remember: just as your parents didn't and couldn't stop you, you won't be able to stop your teenager either.

That being said, let's take it from the teenager's standpoint. When that incident occurs, you need to, at a calm and tranquil moment, remind your parents of this. Then you need to discuss it with them. See if they will reveal what they did. Don't count on it, but I would be curious to find out if they would tell you. I believe that by reminding them they will regress and remember and possibly the next time they might think twice and tend to reason more with the situation.

You, the teenager, also need to understand that there is a different kind of love a parent has for a child than a teenager has for a parent at this stage of your life. In fact, I will bet that there will come a time where you may actually "hate" your parent or parents. Their love for you is something you probably will not fully comprehend until you are, if ever, a parent. This is not meant as an excuse for a parent's behavior. Is is rather an explanation for you, the teenager.

Please take my word for it. It is important that you do. You see, the relationship between a parent and their child and a child for their parent is very, very different. As a teenager think if you will, again at a tranquil moment, what it would be like if one of your parents were deceased. It is a loss for sure. In fact, that will some day happen. But to lose a parent as a teenager when you are in that developmental stage of your life where their nurturing and guidance is really so important to you is without a doubt tragedy.

However, for a parent to lose a child is quite unnatural in the order of things. It is also a hurt that never ever goes away. It is literally a part of you that is lost forever on this plane of existence. It is more so true for a mother. She gave birth to this life and fed it from her breast and nurtured it through the first stages of life. A loss of that magnitude is incomprehensible and incomparable. Trust me on this.

I bring this up because the way you see things now as a teenager will be different when you become an adult. The way you see your parents and what you think of them now will change as you grow and understand more of what life is truly all about. I distinctly remember going to my father at age 28 and telling him how smart he had gotten over the last ten years.

Speaking to the teenager, if you will take a step back in time now and see if you can remember incidents in your life when you were younger at say ten or eight or six years old. See if you can remember what you thought of your parents and what your life was like at that age. I am sure it has changed. It will again, I promise.

In fact, it will almost be a constant change as you grow older and remember what your parents were like at a specific age when you hit those ages of 40, 50 or 60. You will also appreciate them more and what they went through to survive and maintain their status in this ever-changing world we live in.

I am doing a lot of promising here for obvious reasons in hopes some of this will get through to you. While I mean no disrespect in that comment, I just hope you will open your mind to what I am trying to communicate to you, regardless of where you are at in the teenage years.

I promise you, and I know you may not see it now, but you have it easy now as a teenager. There is a lot more responsibility, which brings a lot more pressure and a different type of frustration later on in life when you have to take care of all your own needs. You may say you can't wait for that time because then you will be considered an adult and on your own and not have to answer to anybody. It ain't that easy. But rather than belabor the subject, we'll just let you wait and see. I say this not meaning to be negative but to try to help you *see* that each level of life has its challenges.

First you have to survive the teenage years. Let's face it: you will con-tinue to do what you want to do and what you can get away with regardless of any punishment or grounding because that is your nature at this time. However, the consequences will make you think before you do it and weigh whether it will be worth the satisfaction of whatever it is you intend to do. As I have said before in this book, "There is a price you pay for everything." You decide if it is worth it.

I have not touched on a subject that I think is worth mentioning at your age. This is a truism that should stand out at any age, but definitely as a teenager who is now experimenting with life. That is and I promise you it is true. **Using or participating, even recreationally, with illegal drugs is never, ever worth the price you will pay. Not even if it is only one time. It takes getting caught only one time to totally screw up your life forever. And you have no one else to blame but yourself.** And that is all I am going to say about that.

To the teenager, I wish you the best. You have the opportunity to set the table now. What you do with your life now will have an effect on your future. How will you do it?

If I have in any way helped, please e-mail me and let me know. So says Papa J.

CHAPTER FIFTEEN

THE YOUNG PEOPLE

Here I am talking about the people between the ages of 21 and 35. You are the ones who will shape our Universe and our world for the next 20 years. What you do, how you react and your beliefs will affect the world and this Universe as we know it today.

It is important that our young people *See*. It is important that our young people understand the workings of the Universe.

I speak to you directly. You will be the leaders for generations to come. Our Universe is in a state of change. The movements toward world peace will actually be fulfilled or not by you. It is your responsibility to see that our world survives the terrorism, the global warming, the greed and the corruption that have beset our government and the world powers of today.

It will be your responsibility to see that cures for the diseases that have infected our populations have been discovered and released to the people of the world, regardless of one's financial status. The doctors, lawyers, CEO's, politicians and working force will come from your age group. This is true of the people in all countries, not just the economic and military powers of today. The young of countries like Thailand, Argentina, Taiwan, Nicaragua, Austria, Iran, Egypt and the like. Countries not necessarily known for their economic or military prowess must now step forward as well those who are known and change the world's thinking and attitude if this Universe will make it through to the next century.

It all starts with the individual. It starts by recognizing the power within you and the ability to affect the lives of others in a positive way. It starts with having the vision to *see* what can be done and doing it. It starts small, one person at a time, and then grows like the ripples from a pebble dropped into a lake. It spreads ever endlessly and takes hold.

You need to believe in yourself and your potential. You need to find that purpose which is yours and live it, breathe it, embrace it. You need to create an attitude of self worth for yourself and for those you come in contact with. You must become not only a leader but also and more importantly a teacher.

Considering the changes that have taken place in the last century, I can't even fathom the possibilities that await your generation. What you will do with communications, technology, health and medicine, transportation is overwhelming. The possibilities are endless and beyond me.

Forty years ago I never expected the computer to take over our lives the way it has. I never envisioned cell phone communication to be what it is now. Nor can I foresee where it will go. This is your job now. This is your Universe.

You also need to be very aware of the children that you have and will bring into this world. They will help you to manage our Universe. Learn from them and treat them with the respect that very possibly was not given to you during your lifetime. Learn from the mistakes of your parents.

It is with a great deal of confidence that I write this because from what I *see* the educated parents of today in a greater majority are more aware of their children than those of years past. They do give them more credit for being individuals than those of prior generations. They seem to be more in tune to their offspring and their needs. I believe they are taking the time to nurture and encourage in ways that the prior generation hasn't. There is also a difference in the type and amount of pride they seem to have in their children and their accomplishments.

The family entity is very alive and well in the young parents of today. That's not to say there won't be problems and in some cases divorces, but I believe even then the children won't be left out as was the case when the epidemic of divorce was so prevalent in prior years. Today's parents still keep in touch with their kids and still are an integral part of their lives. Again I know this is a hasty generalization, but it is one I have seen first-hand and believe is part of the change of what is taking place in our Universe. I know there are and will be instances where this is not valid but I truly believe, that in the majority of cases, it is and will be the norm.

We are changing. It is evident if you really look and *see* what is transpiring. The male of our species is taking on more responsibility for raising children. He is taking on more responsibility in household chores. He is finally putting the ego aside, realizing that the family and a marriage is a unit that takes both parties doing their share. It is no longer an entity with the male figure being the so-called "man of the house" and "head of the household" and the antiquated thinking that, "Because I am the man, I am in charge." Women are no longer the subservient species that bend to the whim and fancy of the male.

We have grown up and a marriage is now two people sharing the responsibility of building a life for themselves and raising a family. It is still a tough job, and communication between the parties is more a requirement for a successful marriage than ever before. Today's society requires, more often than not, that both parties hold a job and provide an income so that the family can have the type of life and maintain a standard of living that both desire. In many cases the woman is now making more money than the male. So it was only right and fair that the male come off his perch and share in the other duties to maintain a household.

There is that ego that I mentioned previously. If we can learn to control it, there is no telling what changes can occur and the benefits we can derive by doing so. Fifty years ago this was not the case, but this exemplifies the changes that have taken place in our society.

So you see we have evolved not only technologically but emotionally as well. We are learning to adapt and change. And if we take into consideration the concept of "time," the progress will coincide with the needs of our Universe to survive the crises we have created.

We are not done yet. There is still much to learn and much to change and adapt to, but I believe that we are on our way and it is the young people of this generation who will make it happen. Whatever you do, don't stop now. Continue to seek out answers to questions, continue to learn about the Universe you live in and continue to learn about "The Miracle That Is You."

Papa J has faith in you.

CHAPTER SIXTEEN

KNOWLEDGE

As you can discern from previous chapters, I am not pro-government or pro-establishment. I have seen too much greed, corruption and deceit in my lifetime to trust anyone in a position of power, mainly because power is such an aphrodisiac. The old saying, "Power corrupts; absolute power corrupts absolutely," is so true.

Let me share with you some statistics about our U.S. Congress that I received via email. These are the same people who are creating the laws that are supposed to keep the general public, "US," in line.

Of the 535 members of Congress:
36 have been accused of spousal abuse
7 have been arrested for fraud
19 have been accused of writing bad checks
117 have directly or indirectly bankrupted at least TWO businesses
3 have done time for assault
71 cannot get a credit card because of bad credit
14 have been arrested on drug related charges
8 have been arrested for shoplifting
21 are currently defendants in lawsuits
84 have been arrested for drunk driving in the last year

These are the same people we give lifetime health insurance to when they retire. Need I say more?

Power takes on different shapes and forms. There is Governmental power, which is the most blatant example of corruption and validates the truism. There is parental power. There is social and sexual power. There is medical power, which is another good example. And then there is the power of knowledge. Knowledge is the only power that is a power whether you use it or not. All the other powers have to be wielded to justify and prove that their power exists, but knowledge is an inner power.

If you have the knowledge of how this Universe works and you believe in it, there is a silent confidence that grows inside you. You don't have to foist it upon other people. You don't have to exert it to prove that you have it. You know that you know. Now you can share it with other people and have them benefit from it. You can help other people because you have it and lead them or direct them to the right path.

That knowledge will instill a confidence in you that you will exude to everyone you encounter. There will be a difference in how you see yourself and how others see you. There will be an awakening within you that will bring a smile to your face that emanates from within.

You know that you don't need to worry because everything will work out fine. You know that you are on your path to achieve whatever it is you want from this life. You now will find it easier to *see* and expand upon your knowledge. Others will seek you out and not even know why, just that they know you know something they don't know. They won't even know what questions to ask and will just want to be around you.

But remember: the only life you can control is your own. You can share your knowledge with everyone you meet, but if they don't pick up on it and don't *see,* you can't help them. You can only be a teacher.

There are two quotes that stick in my mind, and I have mentioned them previously but they are worth revisiting. One I attribute to Wayne Dyer, an author I mentioned at the beginning of this book.

The other I attribute to Napoleon Hill, who I have also mentioned before.

The first is "Who is the teacher and what is the message?" the second is "When the pupil is ready, the teacher will appear."

When two or more people get together, one is the teacher and the question is what can we learn or what have we learned from that person. Think about it, and when you sit down with your 20 minutes of self-time, reflect on that. See how it can apply to your life or situation.

The same is true with the second quote. How many times have you heard something and never applied it to your life and then one day you hear the same phrase from someone different and suddenly it strikes a chord and you step back with the attitude. "Yeah, I can see how that makes sense now. Why didn't I see that before?" The answer is that you weren't ready before.

As I grow older I am less pompous about who my teachers are. Twenty-five years ago I knew it all. I just hadn't gotten my break yet. Well, I found out that was a crock of bull. I had a multitude of opportunities and "breaks," but I never saw them.

It's hard to admit to yourself that you were so caught up with the wrong things that you missed your opportunities and worse yet never saw them except in retrospect. This time I am more aware and have a great deal more patience. I am not as caught up trying to attain something I really have no interest in simply to satisfy an inflated ego.

A small example is the job I am working at now. When I first took the job, I was told that supervisors would be offered stock in the company. Well I saw that as my retirement package and that was a goal that I had set and worked towards. I soon found out that it wasn't going to work that way at all.

Now several supervisory positions opened up that I could have applied for and may have gotten. However, I realized that I really didn't want them. I didn't want to devote that much time to this company and be that involved in their politics. So I suppressed my ego and stayed at the position I was in as just a sales agent. I go home when my shift is up. I don't get calls at night or on weekends. I am not running to nonsensical meetings.

I don't have to worry about reports. I just do my job to the best of my ability and sell. I have been employee of the month. I have been top sales agent of the year four times. I have won trips and awards, and I don't have the headaches. I enjoy my time with my family and find time on occasion to do some writing. I am making as much as the supervisors and in some cases more. So what did I need the title for? Years ago I would have fought for that title. Not now.

My opportunities now are of a different nature. The best part is that I know it. Now I find myself learning from everybody. I learn from the kids, teenagers and young adults as well as peers. You can learn from anybody and everybody even if it is only what not to do. Truthfully it is a much more enjoyable world now that I have opened my mind and increased my awareness.

That is why I say don't worry if you missed an opportunity—even if you find yourself, at a time of reflection admitting that you knew about this or that but never applied it to your life. That's okay. You will get another chance, and another chance after that. The Universe will never fail you. *Only you, can fail you,* and then only because you stop trying. As long as you keep on keeping on you have merely had a setback; you have not failed. You will learn from the setback and try again. It is important that you understand that if you have the knowledge and use it correctly, failure *will not be an option*.

113

You see, once you have found your purpose and are living it, you will be in harmony with the Universe and at peace with yourself and will have accomplished what you were put on this earth to do. So you can't be a failure if you have achieved that. It is incontrovertible. ***You are a Success!***

Your purpose, as you see it, may be to get married, have kids and raise them to be contributors to our society and Universe. Your job will be to provide for that family as best you can. It doesn't mean you have to be a millionaire or even making $100,000 a year. You can provide very well for your family by living within your means and on what you earn. You can be very happy and raise very intelligent, well-balanced children who know the love of parents and a family. You can raise children who are taught to respect others regardless of race, religion or creed and taught to respect the Universe they live in. Don't we wish we had a whole country of people like that?

Believe me, that is not an easy thing to do, and it is a feat in my estimation that deserves tremendous recognition and is by definition a person who is a ***Success.***

You see, my father did that. He worked his proverbial butt off to provide for his family, sometimes two and three jobs just to make ends meet. He also loved his family very much and was very proud of us, but he never really enjoyed it as he could have. First, he didn't know how to express love. He didn't know how to give a compliment. He was a tortured soul always looking for the proverbial brass ring. Even when he was starting to lose his faculties to Alzheimer's, he would fantasize about some deal he was putting together that would put him on easy street. Here was a man who worked days and weekends to go to law school at night to become a lawyer and support his parents in the process. And he did. Unfortunately he never understood the Universe and its workings. He never listened to the teachers he met until it was too late and was losing his mind to disease.

He was a brilliant man, but he never got the education (the one you can't buy but you pay for anyway) he needed to put it all together. He never learned how to use his talents. He never learned that he had it all inside him. He never stopped to enjoy what he had in front of him.

I was the apple that never fell far from the tree. My quest was his quest. I also wanted to do it for him. But I too was misguided until I learned what I had inside me and how this Universe works. It was too late for me to teach my father. Two of my teachers were my brother Keith and my sister Gail. They have spent many hours teaching me about the workings of our Universe. Both of them are alternative healers (but that is another book).

I am finding as I am writing this book that the chapters in many ways connect with each other but also are and can be somewhat repetitive. I mention that because I need to go back to certain truths. How far do they reach?

THERE IS NO SUCH THING AS COINCIDENCE

How far can we stretch that? I believe it is a constant in our world. If that is true, let me present a question to you. Is it possible that my sister and my brother and I were born into the same family by design or happenstance?

Play with that one a while and let's move on to the next chapter.

CHAPTER SEVENTEEN

FRIENDSHIP

There is an old saying "If you want a friend, be a friend"

One of the things I have always tried to do is to be there for the people I consider friends. I have tried to help when and how I could. Sometimes that meant lending money. I didn't always get paid back, yet I felt good about doing it. It was sometimes disappointing when they didn't pay back, but then I would look at what the trade off was. What did I get from that friendship? Usually I got as much as I gave and sometimes more. What it did teach me was that you couldn't put a price on friendship. There is no monetary value to it. It's another one of those instances in life where you give and you do get back tenfold. Not always from that person though. It comes back to you in other ways. It is not always an equal trade. It is not always apples for apples. I have been there for people in other ways, too, not just financially.

I heard a great explanation of the difference between rich and wealthy. Shaquille O'Neal the basketball player is rich. The man who pays his salary is wealthy.

And money comes hard to me. It has never come easy. And when it did, somehow I managed to spend it unwisely and so it was gone anyway. I feel I have learned that money isn't everything, and I believe that was what the lesson was. I learned that friendship IS more important than money, that money isn't the most important thing in our Universe. That having a friend that you can share your life and happiness events with is much more important. I invited a couple of friends to a birthday party I was having for my wife Ellie, and a few of them didn't show up or begged out of coming. That really bothered me more than any money I might have lost. I felt like they should have acknowledged how special I thought they were that I invited them by making an effort to come to the party. That was my measure of their friendship.

It was there that I learned the lesson and was able to put into perspective the question about the money.

To me, a friend is someone who cares about you as a person and doesn't judge you or what you do. Now there are extremes that I admit can strain that statement. But I am speaking of the everyday things, not the egregious crimes perpetrated upon another individual. I mean a friend who doesn't judge you for your religion, opinions, preferences, sexual or otherwise. One whose company you enjoy. I remember when I was younger I had friends for different activities. If I wanted to go out to dinner with the wives, it would be one person or couple. If I wanted to go bowling, it would be another person. If I wanted to go bar hopping it would be someone else. And so forth. If I threw a party, I invited them all. It is really still the same now except the activities are different. Now it's movies, maybe golf or to just hang out and throw some steaks on the grill. Some are straight, some are gay, some white, some black or Hispanic. More than one friend had ties to the Mafia.

The friendships vary, but all of them are special to me. I judge none of them, and they do not judge me. I would be there in a heartbeat for any one of them, and in most cases I have at one time. And at times of need they have been there for me, too.

The diversity of my friends keeps me aware of what goes on in the world from extremely different viewpoints, which I find fascinating. It is also quite educational and helps me form my opinion after being able to hear their viewpoints and digest the varied information and determine what seems logical and fair to me.

Sharing the events of your life, good and bad, with other people whether it is family or friends is cathartic. It helps you continue on. Your being and your soul need that release and camaraderie, especially if it's problematic. Now I am not saying give up all your dark secrets. But I am saying to talk about problems if you have them or share your disappointments in this life as well as your successes. That to me is where friends and family can be a big help. It is not so much that you seek or will even get solutions to those problems, but it is good to get them out. Many times, as you talk about them, you will find that the solution comes to you as you hear yourself discuss the situation. Or one may just give you an idea that you will expand upon, and it will solve the problem. As for your successes and happy events and moments, you definitely want to share them with your friends and family. Generally people love to see other people happy and are happy for you. Your happiness and positive energy is then contagious. It also strengthens your positive energy field by doing so.

This also works conversely. If you can find the patience to listen to your friends and family with their problems, you can also share in their successes and be happy for them and reap some of that positive energy that they emit at those times.

As for the negative energy that is emitted at times of trouble, you need to combat that and reassure them that they will find a solution and tell them that you will pray for them and a solution to their problem. Then go do it and reenergize your own positive energy at the same time. You'd be surprised how this actually works for you and for them.

The easiest way to be a good friend is to listen and not judge. Just be a good listener. You will be amazed at how many people you will draw to you by having that trait.

You may also find that many people who you consider friends may be great at telling you their problems but will never be able to or want to listen to you and yours. That's okay. You just be there for them at their time of need, and you will still come out a winner.

Interestingly, I learned this the hard way, too. It was a stressful time in my life, and I was constantly listening to friends and family and their problems and sharing their experiences both good and bad, and no one was listening to me. I found suddenly that I had no friend or family that would just listen to me without turning the conversation back to them.

That's where I learned how easy it is to start out talking about yourself and have the conversation turn to the other person's dilemmas, and yours never gets heard. The conversation ends, and you are frustrated because you never got to say what you wanted to say or discuss. I also realize that I do that to other people on occasion, and then I catch myself and shut up and listen.

The upshot of this was that I ended up going to a social worker and through a bit of therapy. I probably went about five or six times, but what I realized was that I just needed someone to listen to me. I needed someone to devote an hour or more simply to listening to me. I wasn't looking for solutions or answers. Just listen. Now, being trained for that type of situation, she also was able to inject some thought and ask questions regarding our conversation and my rambling diatribe, which I have to admit did help somewhat. Lynn was good at what she did. Once I realized why I was seeing her and that I just needed someone to listen to me, I was able to find people, family and friends to fill that type of need.

The point here is that there are times where we all need help of some sort. It may be professional help; it may just be a friend. It is no shame to admit that. You are no less a person by seeking the help that you need. In fact, I believe it makes you a better individual and is a sign of intelligence and awareness when you realize that no one does it all alone. Everyone, and I mean everyone, needs help along his or her journey through this life.

One of the most important lessons I learned in life was how to be happy for someone else's success and not be the least bit envious.

I had returned to the U.S. after spending a year in Italy. It was by far not a financially productive year; in fact, it was a financial bust for me and for my partners. However, one of the people who was over there with us was quite successful and came back to a brand new home in Florida. This was a man who had been a cab driver in Brooklyn only a few years before and was just beginning to experience financial success in his early 40's. He had had a tough time in Italy health-wise, and we weren't even sure he would make it back. Anyhow, we walked into his new home on a lake and tears were running down his cheeks as he walked through this spacious home. His home. I remember tears coming down my face, too. I was truly happy for him. I never had even one twinge of envy while we were walking through that house. All I could feel was an effervescence of joy for him. That was a lesson I never forgot. I stayed friends with this man until he passed away from cancer many years later.

His was a friendship that was different from many and yet was one I cherished dearly. I have included a poem I wrote about Gennaro and gave to him before he died. In fact, there are two poems at the end of the book on friends and friendship.

I have been truly blessed with many people who I consider friends that have come into and been an integral part of my life. The experiences I have shared with these people are etched in my memory and are a part of what makes me who I am. They have all affected my life in a positive manner. Some of them have already passed away, and I must admit I miss them greatly.

I have found that if you show you care about someone and their problems, they in turn will care about you. If you show genuine affection, you will receive that in return. If you are an honest person and one who respects the truth, you will find that truth will follow you on your journey through this life. If your purpose in this life is to contribute to the welfare of the Universe in whatever manner that is within your means to do so, you will find greater fulfillment and a life that is harmonious with the Universe along with the wealth of peace and contentment within yourself. This outlook and attitude will be the *touchstone* others will draw to and will exemplify *"The Miracle That Is You."*

Friendship and the love that goes with it is a powerful energy in one's life. Partake in it, cherish it, nurture it and never judge and you will be well rewarded. Remember: **To have a friend, be a friend.** So says Papa J.

CHAPTER EIGHTTEEN

YOUR HEALTH

I think at this juncture it is a good time to bring into play my "You're okay" theory.

Our medical society and especially our pharmaceutical society are making millions and millions of dollars from peoples' misery. Does the word d*epression* ring a bell? This condition is probably more prevalent than cancer.

I know I find myself depressed at times and have had several bouts with it in the past. I still fight it. I find myself not wanting to do anything and will sit in front of a TV set and not really watch any specific program. I'll just flick back and forth and through the 300 channels I have on my cable. I have binged out on junk food or found some other way to pass the time and not accomplish anything. Then I beat myself up for not doing what I had planned to do, wanted to do or intended to do. I get down on myself Big Time.

I question why do I do that. Why does my mind go into such a funk that I don't have the desire, or energy, to do anything? I procrastinate on things that I know are important. It doesn't matter what they are, just that I should be doing something to help myself, achieve a goal, go food shopping, do laundry, visit a sick friend. Anything, but nothing. In some cases I don't even want to get out of bed and will wile away a whole morning or day just dozing off and on. Why is that? I know of other people who have it worse than I do. They can spend days or weeks or months in that type of funk.

As a result of that, psychotic medications and diagnoses of depression, anxiety, social disorder are commonplace and the drugs prescribed like Xanax, Prozac, Zoloft, Wellbutrin and the like are even being advertised on television. There are also those medications that are even stronger.

My mother-in-law went through bouts of manic depression and for years was treated with drugs and electro-shock therapy and finally succumbed to pancreatic cancer. There was always a question in my mind if it was not the medications that she was given that eventually led to her cancer and her death at 72 years of age.

We are now finding out that the side effects of those drugs are dangerous, and we don't even know all of them yet. The doctors did admit that she had a chemical imbalance in the brain. What that chemical was or what the imbalance was I don't know, but they couldn't reproduce the chemical or offset the imbalance so this poor lady suffered for over twenty years.

The condition was attributed to an automobile accident she had in her 40's, which caused a concussion and obviously other more severe brain injuries that the doctors could never really determine. When she wasn't going through bouts of depression, she was a vibrant, positive, loving, gracious individual, mother, grandmother and a lady of stature. You never knew when she would fold up or when she would come out of it. It was truly a night-and-day situation. She could be great for months and then wake up and not want to get out of bed or see anyone and stay that way for several months. Then one day she'd wake up and she was fine. Obviously, eventually the drugs worked. And they tried almost every drug available at that time and each time it was a different drug or dosage as the body adjusted to the previous one.

I sometimes wonder whether the diagnosis of "chemical imbalance' isn't just a catch phrase that doctors use because they really don't know what causes this condition and they are compelled to come up with some diagnosis and reason. Thus we'll call it a "chemical imbalance." Without some sort of a label or diagnosis, they cannot prescribe a medication. And then, of course, that means they will lose out on their little kickback from the drug companies.

On the other hand, does the chemical imbalance cause the depression or does the feeling of being down and depressed cause the body to produce or stop producing the chemicals we need to be balanced?

An analogy, if you will. We know that when we feel pain the body can produce chemicals such as endorphins to assist us to cope with that pain. We know that when we eat food the body produces enzymes to help us digest that food. We know that serotonin, which is a chemical of the brain, is also produced at various times. In fact, it is the chemical serotonin that drug companies try to duplicate with their psychotic drugs. Except that the side effects of those drugs are addictive, and I believe they will eventually kill you.

Yet people take these drugs like candy. And then they become so dependent upon them that they can't get off them. The drugs do work for a while. They do help the state of mind. Others fight it and won't take the medications because of the feared side effects and battle the disorders without it, which can be terrifying and frustrating.

So what does one do?

I am not a proponent of psychotic medication. But if I had a case like my mother-in-law I would definitely say, "Hey, whatever works for you." And I say that because we don't yet know enough about the brain and its workings to treat a situation like hers except by the methods we have available to us. Do I believe there is another way? Yes, strongly, but I don't know what it is. Hopefully we will find it soon. The theory of chemical imbalance sounds the most logical because that would indicate a problem with the human body that is obviously malfunctioning. The cure has to be within the body itself or from one like it or in the plants and vegetation on our planet.

I also believe the stress we put on ourselves as we go through life and the frustration we battle trying to achieve what goals we set for ourselves or just trying to make ends meet can and do contribute greatly to these disorders. I believe strongly that the two biggest contributors are the quest for the almighty dollar and relationships.

The quest for money can be extremely frustrating. Is my job paying enough? Will I ever get the house I want, the car I want, enough money to leave this town, city or state that I live in, to feed my family and keep a roof over their heads?

Create your own scenario here, and it will apply. We are a country obsessed with money. Hey! I love it, too, but I believe I have it in a better perspective than I did 20 or 30 years ago.

But the frustration of not having it or having the means to acquire it in the amounts or abundance that you desire or believe that you need or actually need to survive has brought down many a person. It has driven many a person to the office of the "candy man," otherwise known as the doctor. It's easy; the doctor labels you with a disorder of sorts which justifies giving you the medication to help you cope with your problems, and he gets a kickback in some form from the pharmaceutical company for prescribing or dispensing their product. Meanwhile you now have something to calm your nerves. Hey, everybody wins. Right?

Not really! Your problem has not really been solved. You have just been given something to assuage your nerves so you don't harm yourself or someone else. You still have the problem. And now you also have a label on you for the health insurance companies.

Is there a solution? As a concerned layperson and using the logic I have come to rely upon, I believe there is in many cases. Not all cases, but many cases. We will get to that in a moment.

Another factor I believe that can cause these disorders is relationships, whether it is between husband and wife, boyfriend and girlfriend, friends, significant other or life partner, siblings, parents, bosses, coworkers, whatever. It is in essence dealing with another human being.

The people that can affect you the most in a negative as well as a positive manner are your loved ones or someone you love and care for. It is their opinion of you that you care about. It is how they see you that matters. Harsh criticism from those people can easily throw you into a depressed state. Whether that lasts for a few hours, days, weeks or months depends obviously on how you see yourself. If they hit a nerve, which deep down you may already know exists, it can be devastating to your mental balance and ego, which in my opinion is why we have so much domestic violence. The thought of rejection from a loved one just tears at the fabric of your life, which I also believe is a contributing factor as to why we have so many divorces.

It is difficult to accept that we are not perfect and that person not only sees that but has the "audacity" to bring it to the surface by telling you. I mean you know you are not perfect and you know that you have flaws. But for someone you care about to tell you that and then reject you because of that is crushing.

How can someone not want me? I know I am not perfect but neither are they. I am willing to accept their flaws; why can't they accept mine? Besides, I love them and that should conquer all. Well, as we know, it doesn't.

Now it is possible to love someone and not be compatible enough to be able to live with that person in a domestic relationship. When that is realized, it needs to be ended before someone gets hurt. Been there, done that.

There are interesting factors here, which provide the solution to the problem. One is that you are dealing with the energy of another individual, which is negative to you. That means that you have to realize this and change the situation. Easier said than done I know.

The second is that you need to realize that that individual is actually performing a miracle and changing your life. You may not see it that way at the time, but that person is forcing you to do something that you may not want to do but will and should do, and there is a reason for it. The situation is forcing you to change and to move on to the next person, relationship or stop in your life. It may be a job, a move to a different city or place, or to find another person to share your life with. It will be a good thing. It may not seem so at first, but it will. Why would you want to stay at a place or with a person who does not want you there? In a rational moment of thought, isn't it really better for you to move on?

Then there are those who want a relationship so badly that they get depressed because they can't find one for whatever reason. That reason may be physical appearance, or age, or personality problems or just the fact that they have not yet met the individual that is compatible and maybe never will. Why? I can't answer that definitively.

But I strongly believe that there is more than one person who is compatible with you and is good for you and you for them. There has to be. That is the way of the Universe. That is the balance that the Universe provides.

It may well be that you are in the wrong place to meet that person. Listen, we all make choices that affect and direct our lives. Try connecting the dots. You may see that you had an opportunity to do something or go somewhere and didn't do it for whatever reason. In doing so you should get an intuition when you hit that point in your exercise. There should be some type of movement within you. If so, revisit that scenario and see if that might now be a consideration. If the intuition is strong enough I would consider making that change. If not, ask the Universe to send to you that person with whom you are compatible or to give you the direction as to where you need to go to meet that person. What have you got to lose?

Remember: You can control only *your* life. If things didn't work out here, then there is something better for you at the next stop whatever that may be. It doesn't do you any good to dwell on it, get depressed and let this person or situation get and take control of your life. I am in no way minimizing the effect it has on you, your ego, your financial wherewithal, or your life. I promise you I know it hurts ***BIG TIME.***

But I also know that there is something better waiting for you if you will drum up a positive outlook after you have gotten over the hurt. If you will persevere, you will succeed. The Universe will help if you ask it to and then be aware and have the patience and fortitude to deal with the disappointment and the hurt. I swear to you it works

The other and most important point to be made in all cases dealing with depression, anxiety, so called social disorders is that ***YOU ARE OKAY.*** What I mean by that is don't worry, you are okay. It is ***OKAY*** to get down and depressed. You are not an evil or bad person. You are not an incurably sick individual. Don't wish yourself to die. Don't wish yourself to find an escape. (This may sound ridiculous, but I will explain further later)

You have had a traumatic experience or have had a down day or have had a frustrating time trying to achieve a goal. Or maybe you are just stressed out from dealing with life and need a break. ***Don't worry; you're okay.***

You need to recognize what has happened, is happening or will happen. If you take your twenty minutes and reflect, you will probably be able to connect the dots and see what went wrong. It can be extremely obvious or maybe it is a bit more elusive. But I believe that you can find what triggered your depression. And just in case you don't, don't worry; that is okay, too. You will come out of it. Eventually you will come out of it. I believe in many cases people drive themselves further into the depressed state because they worry about it or they beat themselves up for being this way. It's okay.

Work through it. Give it time. In a sense, succumb to it. Let the depression run its course, again knowing it is only temporary. Don't fight it and don't cause yourself any more angst over this state of mind then need be. If you can, enjoy it. Sounds crazy, but let it go. If all you feel like doing is staying in bed, do so. If all you want to do is to watch TV, then watch TV. Whatever it is that you want to do (without hurting yourself or someone else), give in to it and take your mind elsewhere. The key is not to feel any guilt over doing this and not to beat yourself up because of it. Admit to yourself that this is what you are going to do and you are okay with it. If it really has that strong a hold on you, don't fight it. Try this. What have you got to lose?

Most of what I have heard about depression and those who have it is that they are overwhelmed by people who don't have it offering solutions that usually are not right for the people that do. I know what works for me. I know I come out of it sooner and I have less angst over the whole incident. I also feel I have earned that time to just let it all go. Another possibility, which I have found to be successful, is as follows.

If you can, find what I call a happy place. Find a memory or two or three in your life where you were extremely happy. Find one of those moments where you experienced that warmth from deep down erupting though your system and ending up with a smile on your face and a happy tear in your eye. Maybe it was the birth of a child when you held that precious life in your arms for the first time, a wedding day or special romantic interlude, a day when you excelled at sports or received recognition on a job.

Perhaps it was a moment with a loved one that was exhilarating and touching. Maybe a prideful day like your child's graduation or a performance they gave. Then bring yourself back to that moment. Relive it. Really go back and recall and relive that feeling and experience. Your mind remembers, and the emotions are still there if you will ask for the recall. Then let that moment take you to another moment. And another. Then reflect on how lucky you really are to be you. You really are a great person, and there is a lot to like about you and love about you. You just need to believe it. You just may find yourself out of the depressed state, at least for a while.

There is an exercise my brother told me about where you sit in a quiet place alone and you chant to yourself. "I love me, I love me, I love me." While you do this, you let your right hand tap your right leg emphasizing each word and then let your left hand tap your left leg the same way. Do that for about two minutes. You can repeat the exercise with "I am a good person." You can actually do this with any phrase. Just make sure it's positive.

What you are doing is the right hand tapping contacts the left side of your brain and the left hand the right side. In doing this you are getting the attention of both sides of the brain and filling it with positive reinforcement in your own behalf. No negative thoughts have the opportunity to creep in there to dispel anything you are doing. The next time you go to beat yourself up for something that you did, your brain will automatically respond with I love me or I am a good person or whatever message you put in there.

Obviously this is not something you do just once and you forever love yourself. Like anything else, you want to practice this technique daily if possible. And be sincere when you say it. Say it with feeling and emotion. Believe it when you say it. It does work.

On a different note, I took a Dale Carnegie course many years ago and one of the books that was required reading was entitled <u>How To Stop Worrying and Start Living</u>. The prescription for worry was to ask the question "What is the worst thing that could happen?" Other than death, of course, because then you wouldn't have any worries.

If you can accept the worst and figure out what you would do if the worst occurred and what your way out of the worst would be, then you could work on improving the situation, so the worst doesn't occur. As we know, the worst very rarely happens. And if it does you have already figured out a plan. So don't worry. You will work it out. That's part of being the Miracle that you are.

You know with depression that you eventually will come out of it. Whether you have to take medication or just work your way out of it doesn't matter. Know that in time whether it is an hour, a day, a week or a month, you will come out of it. And when you do, this time you will *realize* that it was a temporary state and the next time it occurs you will have *the knowledge* that this is only temporary. It will be a very comforting feeling having that knowledge, and I believe that it will shorten the time frame the next time it happens.

Regardless of the time frame, you need to accept yourself and who you are along with all your frailties and your attributes. If you aren't willing to accept yourself, how can you ask anyone else to accept you?

This is who you are. This is what the Universe created. The Miracle *is* you. You can perform miracles. Because you are, you are a note in the Grand Symphony of life. You are important. You have a purpose here. When you discover what that purpose is, you will find peace and harmony, which will bring contentment and happiness.

Even with all this knowledge you will sometimes break down. The strange thing about depression is that, while you may not know how to help yourself and may not be able to function as you want to, you will still be able to help others and perform your miracles. Somehow we find the strength to do that with the people we come into contact with regardless of our own state of mind. Then we go back home to our depression. Why is that? Think about that and realize that state of mind is only temporary. The Universe is showing you that.

Now I am not saying, don't get or try to get help for depression. By all means exhaust whatever resources you can find to help you. Many times if it is a chemical imbalance medication can help. What I am saying is that it is a condition or in some cases it is classified as an illness, but very often it can be controlled and more often than that it is temporary. The most important thing is don't beat *yourself* up over being depressed. Think of it if you will, as *this is part of the uniqueness that is you.* You are still a note in the Grand Symphony of life and this Universe. You are still, can be and will be, a productive member of our Universe. You can still perform Miracles and *YOU* are still a *MIRACLE*

The same is true of every other problem you encounter. It is a temporary situation. You will work through it. You will find a way out of any dilemma you encounter. You need to draw strength from the knowledge you have and have accumulated and believe in the Universe that is guiding you. In your reflection time ask the Universe, "WHY?" Ask for help, and you will see the Miracles unfold. Stay aware and have the patience to allow the Universe to work its magic.

Even for those who were displaced during Katrina's onslaught will in most cases find better lives for themselves and for their families. Yes, they have tougher times ahead. I don't discount or minimize that. I still believe that they will be better off than they were before Katrina hit. I would love to be able to revisit those people five years from now and see where they are in their life. Hopefully, someone will take on that task.

While on the subject of depression and the mind, I have an interesting theory and I question whether our medical profession has ever investigated the possibilities. Is there a link between depression, stress and Alzheimer's?

I personally know three men who have been diagnosed with Alzheimer's, my father, my father in-law and my brother in-law. In all three cases they went through a period of extreme personal stress for a long period of time prior to being diagnosed with the disease.

My father was constantly distraught at not being able to make the type of living he wanted, to provide my mother the standard of living he wanted for her and at the same time adapt to a changing world that had left him behind. He was so stressed that even after he was diagnosed he would frequently create these fantasies of business deals that he was working on to achieve that end. His first symptoms were at around age 70 and he died at age 84.

My father-in-law was living with the stress of my mother-in-law's depression for over 20 years and had to find some escape during the times that she was in a depressed state, which as I mentioned previously could be for three, five or six months at a clip. And it could occur without warning and would happen every couple of years or so. His symptoms were noticed in his late 70's and he died at age 84.

My brother-in-law was a closet gay who never did come out. He was a proud individual who was a professor in a college and a teacher in middle schools and was afraid to let that side of him surface for fear of losing his job and the personal embarrassment he felt because of it. So he kept it secret, and it wasn't until he was diagnosed that we began to find the signs verifying what we had suspicions of for many years. His symptoms surfaced at age 64. He is as of this writing living in an Alzheimer's facility.

In each of these cases there was tremendous personal stress on individuals who did not know how to cope with their frustrations or situations or mental and emotional crises. And I am convinced there was a state of depression although it was never diagnosed in either case. Considering the amount of stress they were under it had to be a factor. Perhaps because it was not diagnosed as "clinical depression" it was never considered. Now if depression causes a chemical imbalance or even vice versa can this trigger another chemical imbalance and cause Alzheimer's?

I ask the question: Is it possible that an individual can drive himself or herself to an Alzheimer's state over a period of time? Can the pressure that is put upon us or that we put upon ourselves contribute to or even cause this dreaded condition?

Now we have no idea what causes this disease. Supposedly we have tests, which can detect the condition at early stages. But we cannot stop the deterioration of the brain nor can we determine how long it will take to totally shut down.

Is it not possible that your desire for escape from depression or life itself given to the subconscious mind which acts upon your thoughts and energy could and would obey your command to escape and thus find Alzheimer's to be a solution to the problem? The relativity of good and bad is not a judgment that is made by the subconscious mind. Rather its job is simply to find the answer and respond to your request.

There have been cases where people have willed themselves to die. Their bodies have shut down causing death. That order was given to the brain and the subconscious mind, which acted upon that request, eventually shutting down the body. Why then wouldn't it act in the same fashion to shut down the brain if so requested?

In my father's case, there was evidence that he had had more than one mini-stroke. In my father-in-law's case, he was operated on for blockage in his carotid artery. In my brother-in-law's case, for years he would use aerosol inhalers to clear his sinuses and the part of the brain that is affected with Alzheimer's is right above the sinus area. Could each of these extenuating circumstances also have contributed to the onset of the disease?

Of all the organs of the human body, the brain is the most important, the most complicated and the one we know the least about. Let's face it, the brain runs the whole ship.

I raise the questions and if anyone has a response please feel free to contact me through my website. I don't believe that this is something that has been investigated, and if it has, I haven't seen any articles indicating this. If it has not, doesn't it bear looking into? I presented that question and scenario to an Alzheimers expert and her reaction was that she knew of no studies on that and admitted that it bore looking into and had some merit.

Now that I have that out of my system, let's look at the chemical imbalance theory. I have read articles that theorize that an under active thyroid can cause a chemical imbalance that can lead to depression and other diseases. Hypothyroidism and hyperthyroidism can be responsible for many problems that doctors for some reason will not look for or connect to ailments that could be related or that other studies have indicated are related. Not just depression and Alzheimer's, but other chemical imbalances as well.

We know so little about this type of ailment, and I am of the mind that drugs won't cure it. Basically all drugs do is give our bodies time to fight whatever disease or ailment we have. In many cases the side effects of the drugs are worse than the cure.

I bought and read a book entitled <u>Reversing Diabetes</u> by Julian Whittaker.
There are foods that can help and vitamins that can help. All coincide with my theory that there is a natural cure for the maladies that we have, which is provided by the Universe that we live in. This all coincides with my belief that this finely tuned instrument we call our body was constructed in such a manner that if we break down one part of it or neglect to give it the proper nutrients it needs to function at its optimum, we will pay the price with disease and illness.

Now, am I perfect with this? Hell, no! Do I follow all the rules? Hell, no! I am just learning about all this now. I have made a drastic change in my own lifestyle and will continue to do so. I have changed my eating habits and lost 30 pounds. I have started to exercise more, and by the time this book is published I will hopefully have stopped smoking. Now that is a lot for me, and I know I sound weak when I use the word hopefully. Admittedly, part of me wants to and the other isn't so sure. But regardless of what I do, do this for yourself. I never claimed to be a saint, nor am I a hypocrite. I said before that I have my weaknesses and frailties just like everyone else. I have my Achilles heel. Yes, I am telling you to do things I didn't do and some of the things I probably won't do. Does that make me wrong in what I believe and what I am telling you to do? I don't consider it hypocritical because I am admitting to you up front that what I do is not necessarily in every case what I should do. Am I wrong in not doing it? Yes, I am. Does that mean that you shouldn't do it or investigate the alternative possibilities to protect yourself and your body? You answer that question.

You can start by checking out a website for www.drdavidwilliams.com. Yes, it is a commercial website. Hey, we all have to make a living. But I believe in his theories and have seen them work for myself. More importantly and the reason I recommend you at least take a look at it is that I have known about him for at least 15 years. While I initially never did anything about his advice, I am now and finding more and more that his stuff makes sense. It supports my belief that most of the problems we have today, and the fear that has been created by the pharmaceutical companies and the medical establishment can be remedied by using the natural substances provided for us by the Universe. Also check out, if you will, www.cold-fx.com.

Another reason I so strongly believe in that statement is that, if it were not true, the FDA and pharmaceutical companies and the AMA wouldn't be working so hard and utilizing their militaristic tactics to put these people out of business to suppress this information. As Shakespeare said, "Thy doth protest too much."

What I am trying to do is point out that there are other ways and methods of thinking, of taking care of yourself, of healing yourself, of looking at life and the way you live it, of looking at yourself and understanding the power you have within you.

The Miracle "Is" you.

I beseech you to go further than I and seek out the answers for yourself. Open your mind and *See. See* beyond the norm. *See* beyond what the so-called establishment is trying to sell you. *See* that the fears they are propagating are not real. Question and seek the truth for yourself.

I have not touched on those diseases that happen before birth. There are so many ailments that our children are born with, and we have no cure for them; for instance, Downs Syndrome and Autism.

And even with Autism, which is very much on the rise today, there is a connection to our intake of food and the poor nutritional habits we practice. I didn't forget this situation. I again believe strongly that this is where stem cell research will come into play. I believe that cures will be found for those crippling diseases like cerebral palsy and muscular dystrophy and Lou Gherig's disease.

It just makes sense to me. It is logical to me based upon our creation and based upon the intricacies of the human body. Compare it if you will to one of today's computerized automobiles. It still needs the fluids—gas, oil, brake fluid, power steering fluid and water to run. Take away any one of these liquid compounds and it malfunctions. It has its own computer brain, which ties it all together. It has brake pads and shocks and ball joints and all these small parts, which can wear and break down, and we put it in the hospital for cars.

Then we have the car doctors that we call mechanics. Do you trust them? When you go to a repair shop with this annoying little noise in your car do you find out it will cost $200, $600 or a $1000 dollars to fix it? Do you believe them? Don't you feel that they just upped your bill because you don't know what's wrong with your car? And how many times after you have paid the bill do you find that stupid annoying noise is still there? So back you go to find that it was something else, but those parts that were replaced were worn and needed changing. It just didn't cure that little stupid annoying noise. And now the bill is another $100, $300, $500 or however much it costs. And you pay it because you need your car. You may never go back to that mechanic again, but you pay the bill.

Now really, are doctors much different? You go in with a pain, and they give you a drug or you have surgery. You find out that you still have the pain or with a drug you find out the side effects are worse than that little pain you had.

Am I exaggerating? You tell me. How many times have you gone to a doctor, and after the medication, which nowadays is not cheap, you find the problem still exists? So what happens? You go back and the doctor prescribes another medication. If that doesn't work, there is always another. Doesn't it make sense to see what else is out there? Shouldn't you be putting as much time, effort, investigation and research into curing and helping your body as you would your car?

Your body is a whole lot more complicated than even one of today's automobiles, and there is no manufacturer's manual to go to for repairs. There are no after-market or even manufacturer's parts to purchase to make it well and cure it. There is just one of each part for your body.

Don't you think it deserves more care than your car? Don't you think that it is just a bit more important that it function as properly as your car? Do you really believe that your doctor or any doctor for that matter knows everything he or she needs to know about *your* body to guarantee you will be fine after he or she finishes treating you?

Am I crazy? Are my suggestions and ideas and beliefs crazy? Are my suppositions crazy? Very possibly! What I try to do here is provoke thought. In any way I can. It still comes down to one thing.

It is your body. It's your mind. It's your responsibility to take care of it and guard what you put into it. It is your responsibility to find out everything you need to know to make sure that it is around for as long as you want it to be. And it is your responsibility to start that process NOW. Don't do what I did. Do what I say. I promise you will be better off. So says Papa J.

CHAPTER NINETEEN

LIVING WITH ABUNDANCE AND FREE WILL

I chose to title this chapter specifically to point out the differences of "living with abundance" based upon where you live and what measuring stick one uses to calculate what "abundance" means to them.

I will also in this chapter step on the toes of the religious establishment, big time. Again I know I will hear about this, but that is good. It means people are thinking. It also means I have touched a "hot button," and my interest in doing so is to point out another way to prove that *YOU* are the miracle.

I spoke of our Creator being a *"loving God"* and of our having *"Free Will."* The question always arises, especially when a natural disaster occurs like the tsunami that hit Asia, and Hurricane Katrina that wiped out the city of New Orleans.

If we have such a *"loving God,"* why does the creator allow such tragedies to wreak such terrible havoc on portions of the Universe and kill such large numbers of people? I've heard people blame our Creator for these catastrophes. "Why does God let these things happen? Why doesn't God stop these horrific tragedies?"

You could ask the same question about the ethnic cleansing going on in Africa where hundreds of thousands of innocent men, women and children, are being slaughtered. You could ask the same question about Hitler's killing of 6 million Jews and others during the Holocaust. Or consider Saddam Hussein's gassing his own people. Why didn't the Creator stop that or prevent it from happening? In truth, I don't have a definitive answer but I have a perspective, which I will share with you. It involves my theory on *"Seeing" and "Free Will."*

There is a tribe called the Mokens from the islands off Thailand. They were featured on the TV program 60 Minutes in August 2005. They are a poor people by our standards and live off the sea and the land. They are considered "Boat People." Because the sea and the workings of it is their life, they were aware of the tides and were able to pick up on the abnormal changes prior to the tsunami's hitting their land. The oldest of their tribe warned the younger people and was able to convince them to head for high ground. Those who didn't listen paid the price. Those who did heed his warnings were spared and learned a lesson that they will pass on to future generations.

Those who were lounging on the beaches and at the resorts of Thailand never saw the signs and made no move to higher ground. Now I have never experienced a tsunami and never want to. But the pictures and movies taken give evidence to a natural disaster that is a phenomenon of Nature that is overwhelming in power and awesome in scope. But there were signs. How many people would have had the time to get out even if they did recognize those signs, I don't know. But there were signs, and had we the knowledge of those signs and the knowledge or the experience of what measures to take, we might have been able to at least reduce the number of casualties. Truly we were not paying attention. Like it or not, it is a fact. I am not blaming anyone. Had I been there, I seriously doubt that I would have been a survivor, but we had warning.

As an aside, do you think it might be a good idea to include these happenings and the warning signs in the curriculums of our high schools and colleges? Would it be a good idea to teach our kids of the dangers of the catastrophes that Mother Nature can wreak upon our Universe and what they must do to avoid being one of the statistical casualties. What say you?

The hurricane that destroyed New Orleans in August, 2005 and left hundreds of thousands in devastation was a terrible tragedy. The levees that broke (there is now a theory that those levees were actually blown up by our own government to protect the other levees in place and the resulting casualties were termed collateral damage.) and flooded the city along with the Category 4 winds of 145 miles per hour left hundreds of thousands of people homeless and without food and water. The numbers are just staggering; and having experienced three of the hurricanes that hit Florida in 2004, I can empathize and sympathize with those people, and my heart goes out to them.

But we must note here that it was our government and the Mayor of New Orleans and the Governor of Louisiana who failed the people of that city, too. They have known for close to 40 years that those levees would not hold up to a Category 4 hurricane. It was no big surprise when the levees broke (if they truly did). The Government's worst fears were far exceeded by Hurricane Katrina.

You also must consider that New Orleans was a city built 25 miles below sea level with bodies of water on two sides. It was really no surprise to the powers that be that they were buried under a deluge. The government of Louisiana had at least 48 hours to prepare transportation to evacuate the city. The Federal Government did not take action to help those people until five days after the tragedy occurred.

Now some people did get out and were able to save their lives—maybe not their property, but they can rebuild. Obviously the people that are hurt the most after one considers the loss of life are the people who had little to begin with and now have less than nothing. Those people have to wonder where their next meal is coming from for themselves and for their children.

It has to be a terrifying experience, and I am not in any way undermining or minimizing the tragedy and its effects on the city, the state and the Universe as a whole.

However, I must also point out that there are people who are living in California who know they are living on a fault line that could result in an earthquake that could destroy their city and their way of life in no less a tragedy than the one that occurred in New Orleans. Is this any different from the people who chose to live in a city 25 miles below sea level?

It's not different from the people living on the coastal beaches and cities in Florida and not different from the people living in the Midwest who are prone to tornadoes and draughts. The people living in the north and northeast deal with bitter cold winters and snow storms that cripple their way of life for days on end each year.

Every country in the world has had its natural disasters resulting in catastrophic destruction and loss of life and property. We can go back in history and see similar incidents. The point here is that we know it will happen. We don't always know where or when, although in today's society we have a lot more knowledge of where and when than ever before, especially when it comes to hurricanes. The most irresponsible note is that we rarely prepare, even with all the experience and knowledge that we have. We didn't and don't learn from our history.

While I feel greatly for the victims of these happenings, I can't in my mind blame the Creator because we have warnings or knowledge of what can happen. As cold-hearted as it may seem, we have *chosen* to make our homesteads in these areas. It is akin to "pick your poison," and then we must deal with the consequences of *our choices*.

I believe a system was created for this planet. When man arrived, he was compelled to deal with and live within that system. We have progressed tremendously in the last hundred years and will progress immeasurably more in the next hundred years. We may even learn to harness the energy brought on by these natural happenings, and hopefully some day we will find the means technologically to be able to warn the people of this Universe and be able to prepare for these devastating occurrences. Whether the people will heed those warnings is another story.

This is a great part of what I allude to when I use the word *"Seeing."* It refers to being aware totally of what is around you, not only regarding people but with your surroundings as well. Being aware of the system of Nature as well as the people. Being aware of the energy around you location-wise, too.

I know you have heard stories of buildings and houses being haunted. I know I have walked into a building or a house and just had an eerie feeling. I couldn't put my finger on it as to why but it was something I just felt. I was not comfortable in that place. I can't say that anything ever really happened there, but I didn't really stay that long either. I got out as soon as possible. I can't even relate to you of an occurrence after I left. It was just that "something."

I have come to learn to pay attention to those intuitions, because they serve me well in so many other situations. So when I feel something isn't right, I change the circumstances. If that means leaving, I do.

We are still learning about the workings of our Universe. There is so much we still don't know and so many questions still unanswered.

Now I have mentioned and somewhat got into the term *"Free Will."* I bring this up now because it is part of my perception of why we were created, what our purpose is, and it also ties in with the statements I made previously in this chapter.

I believe we have *"Free Will"*; I believe it is the makeup of who we are and what we can do. I also take the term very literally. If you do take it literally, then certain constants must apply.

If you believe that you have *"Free Will"* given to you by our Creator, then you can do anything you want to do and there can be, and is, no judgment by God. Now please read that last sentence again. If God gave us *"Free Will,"* then there are no other rules. There can be no other rules. Once you implement a rule of any kind, *"Free Will"* ceases to exist. So it is all or nothing. I believe it is all.

Any laws, any restrictions, to that have been installed and implemented by man. We know that for century's religion and the "fear of God" has been force fed to us mainly to keep us in line. It is amazing to me how well it has worked. Our religious leaders have and were able to brainwash us to the point where we did some ridiculous and inane penances simply to pay retribution for the sins we committed that were in reality never acknowledged as such by a "loving God."

These religious leaders were able to manipulate our minds and way of thinking for their own purpose, which in some cases was financial greed and other cases for the power that went with the position.

With a "loving God" and *"Free Will,"* it means that there can be no Hell, only heaven, which means that everyone who lives and dies will end up in heaven as such, or in the place our souls go to once they leave this physical vessel they are housed in. There can be no sins or sinners by God's standards, only by man's standards.

That means we do have a "loving God." We have a God that loves every individual, every soul, every living thing, equally, regardless of what that individual or soul or living thing has done while alive and here on this Universe.

Jeffrey J. Halperin

That means that Hitler, Mussolini, Idi Amin, Saddam Hussein, Geoffrey Dahmer, Osama Bin Laden and every other tyrant, murderer or SOB that you know or have heard of will be as welcome when their souls leave their body as was Mother Theresa.

I don't mean to denigrate or insult any religion. My intention is not to affront any house of worship or anyone's version of the Bible, Koran, Torah, Kabbalah, or any other religious text. My opinion is that, those texts were written by man. Those texts were written in languages foreign to us and translated into the many languages of the many societies that make up our Universe. Those texts were written or rewritten hundreds or even thousands of years after the incidents that they supposedly occurred.

What little I learned about the Hebrew, Spanish and Italian languages, I do know that there are phrases that, when translated to English, are not literal translations. In some cases, if you do take the literal translation, it totally changes the meaning of the phrase or word that you are trying to translate.

Interestingly enough, in the Moken language there is no word for *"Want."* So how do you translate it?

Consider that the Biblical manuscripts were all translated from different languages (or redone because of erosions and decay so many years after they were originally written), and then consider the fact that our English, or if you prefer, American language has had words or phrases added to it and accepted for our updated dictionaries. I am sure we are not the only country or society to ever do that.

Spanish and Italian, along with French, are derivatives of the Latin language. That word "derivative" means taken from. Taken from suggests that there were additions or deletions. If it were exact it, would be called Latin. But it is called Spanish, Italian or French.

146

They are termed to be "the Romance languages." Each of those languages is similar, but they are distinctly different. How many dialects do we have in each of those languages?

Now the scrolls and Torah were written in Hebrew. How many dialects does the Hebrew language have? Which one was used when it was translated into Latin? Was it translated from Latin into French or Italian or Spanish first? Or were all three translated directly from the Latin version and then to English?

My questions now ask, "How can one so literally accept as dogma this book that was written and translated and translated and translated again, under the circumstances and conditions as I just described?" "How can you say that that book is the literal Gospel from our Creator?" "How can you disprove or refute what I say?" You really can't.

I have said that in the case of my own writing I believe that a force outside of my being has guided me. I even concede that those who wrote the text of the Bible were also guided. But these are also my opinions and my perception of what I was being guided to write. And if the same truth is applied to the text of the Bible, we have one man's written word and perception.

So this is where blind faith comes to fore. This is where people get indoctrinated during childhood and have the "fear of God" instilled. They forever believe in and live by the "Good Book." Depending upon which religion you choose will depend upon which one of the "Good Books" you will get, as there are several versions of it. And the Pastors and Reverends and Priests and Rabbis and Monks and Ministers and the Clergy, men and women, from all the different faiths preach to you about their "Good Book."

That's not so bad until a person who does puts you down and ridicules you for not believing the way they do. When one who does, promotes hate and sometimes death because you are different or believe differently from what he does. It's when one who does is so closed minded that he or she cannot and will not accept the fact that we have *"Free Will."*

In my mind, if you are going to accept a literal translation of something, accept that. Believe what you want. But don't debase someone who doesn't see it your way.

People talk about, believe in and pray to Jesus. Now, I wasn't alive when he was around, and I have difficulty accepting everything people have attributed to him, but three things stick out in my mind that were attributed to him. One of them was that he supposedly stated that, "We are capable of doing all that he has done and greater things." Another is that we have *"Free Will."* The third is to "love thy neighbor as thyself." That makes sense, and if you take that as literally as people have taken everything else in the "Good Book," we would have a changed world.

I seriously doubt that Jesus would condone "an eye for an eye" type of existence. I am sure that Jesus wouldn't promote the hate or call for the elimination or persecution of any group of people or sect regardless of who they are, what they have done, or what their preferences are. Again *"Free Will."* *As* I said, with a loving God there are no exceptions.

Please don't get me wrong; I am not putting down religion. I AM putting down hypocrisy. I AM putting down the people who say, "Thou shalt not kill" on Sundays and practice an "eye for an eye." I AM putting down those who say, "Love thy neighbor as thyself" except for the Jews, Gays, Blacks, Hispanics, etc.

I became extremely disillusioned with organized religion when I listened to a Rabbi stand on a pulpit and wish for the death of Yasser Arafat. I became disillusioned when scandals hit: scandals of the pedophile Catholic priests and the scandals of Jim Bakker and Jimmy Swaggart. And the Imam's of the Muslim faith proclaim a jihad against Americans and others. And the ministers and reverends that stand up and preach against the gays and other people and use the Bible for their own gain and twisted purpose and agenda. These are supposed to be our leaders and show us the way of God and the Creator.

I am very confident that neither Jesus nor Mohammed nor Buddha nor a "loving God" would ever say and do such things. I am also confident that there would be nothing in their "Good Book" that would in any way persecute one of their creations or a sect of people regardless of their preferences, race, color or creed. That is the law of *Free Will*. I am not against religion, but I am against those who misuse the principles and the power we give them.

But then my faith in people is restored when I see what happens when a disaster hits somewhere in the world. Have you ever looked at the scene after one of the tragedies or natural disasters occurs? The whole world seems to band together and become the loving people that God created. People from all over the Universe, from different countries, different religions, races and creeds suddenly put aside their differences and "GIVE" of themselves and their possessions and their time to help those in need. People from all walks of life and professions give. People that have, and those that don't, still find a way to help.

It's at this time of crisis that the true instincts of most people created by a loving God surface and show that they are truly a child of the Creator and a loving God. How many lives do you change? How many miracles do you perform? How far-reaching are those miracles? Will the people you touch ever forget? Will they not tell those stories for generations to come?

Believing in a credo is good. It gives you something to hang onto when a crisis occurs in your life or when hope seems lost. My credo is to believe in the workings of the Universe, a loving Creator and the Miracle that is me.

My credo is to use the *"Free Will"* I was given to better my life, my family's life and the Universe I live in. And to try as best I can to live by the Golden Rule, whoever created it, which is "to treat others as I would like to be treated." I will also try to the best of my ability to obey the man-made laws of this society. I mean, let's face it; jail is not a fun place to be.

What does this all have to with abundance you ask? After all we have gone through, abundance is really an abstract. It is in your mind and whatever definition you choose to put on it. Is it a home and a car? Is it two homes and two cars? Is it a good family and the ability to provide for that family? You decide!

The lesson is to learn to live like you already have it. Then go ahead and improve upon your situation if you choose to do so. With the Moken's who live off the land and the sea, if they have a roof over their head, more than enough to eat, clothes on their back, a family and maybe some friends, they seem to live a life that is full and one of abundance.

During the program two boat loads of friends and relatives came by unannounced, and they broke out and cooked what food and shared what drink they had and they partied as such. I mean, cell phones were not part of their world. They seemed content and happy. I don't believe any one of them would be happy living in my home. It's not their style.

Some people believe that having too many things complicates their lives. I know many people who are wealthy and are so afraid of someone taking advantage of them because they are so wealthy that they actually have trouble sleeping at night worrying about it. They also worry about keeping up with their peers and how they are going to maintain such a high standard of living as well as the desire to buy more of life's toys.

Conversely if you asked one of the people made homeless by Hurricane Katrina, I am sure he or she would feel quite fortunate to have a roof over his or her head and food to eat along with running water and electricity.

Thirty-three years ago I was working in Italy, and one of the people I was working with invited me to his home for dinner. It was in a little town named Avellino, which years later was totally destroyed by an earthquake. But that night two other colleagues and I sat down for dinner with Alfonso and his mother and brother. The house was made of stone and marble. There was no insulation or air-conditioning, so the summers were hot and the winters were cold, as Avellino was situated up in the mountains outside the city of Rome. That night was cool, but the kerosene heater warmed the room. There was a kitchen and dining area and a couple of bedrooms. The home was sparsely furnished, but they were able to find chairs for everyone to sit on around the dinner table. The meal consisted of a soup and a potato and tuna fish salad and homemade Italian bread. Oh and the best homemade white wine I have ever drunk in my life.

At the end of the meal, his mother was crying and I asked Alfonso why. He said that she was embarrassed that she couldn't prepare a better or more traditional meal with the pasta and meat, etc. I went up to his mother and hugged her and told her in my best, broken Italian that this was the best meal we had had since we had been in Italy. The food was delicious, the wine was superb and, most importantly, she welcomed us into her home with warmth and love as if we were family. How could any meal, anywhere, surpass that? She looked up at me wiped away the tears and thanked me. I told her, "No, we thank you."

It was a lesson I never forgot. Here was a mother who wasn't trying to impress anyone, as much as she might have wanted to. She was just sharing with strangers what little she had and did it with love. I saw Alfonso only once after we left Italy some thirty-odd years ago, but I never forgot that evening I spent with him and his family. That was a wonderful evening and a Miracle for me.

It never ceases to fascinate and amaze me how people who have the least are so ready to share what little they have. And with no strings attached.
I may not have as many toys or as nice a house as many other people who are wealthier than I am, but trust me. I live a life of abundance and have a lot more than many of those people will ever have.

Do you want to know what one of the best feelings in life is? It is to set a goal and achieve it. I don't care what the goal is if it is worthwhile for you and you achieve it. It creates a feeling of euphoria within you that is unmatched by anything else. It is what I term "getting high on life."

The same thing happens to you when you realize that you know what your purpose is and have or will create the life that you want for you, that you love yourself and you are happy with who you are.

Hey! I really am a great person. I am a Miracle! I performed a miracle today. It's all a state of mind that you must believe in yourself and the Universe.

The answer, dear readers, is the same for "abundance." It is a state of mind. You decide what it is for you. So says Papa J.

CHAPTER TWENTY

WHERE DO WE GO WHEN WE DIE?

There are various and a multitude of theories. The Christians and Catholics believe in a heaven and hell. The Muslim extremists believe that it is better to die a martyr and get to the promised land as soon as possible. The Buddhists believe that you are reincarnated based upon your Kharma in this life.

I have a friend, George, who believes that when we die, that's it. There is nothing else after that. It is over. Finished. Done. His theory is that man's ego is so strong that he refuses to acknowledge that when he dies there is nothing else. He believes that man cannot accept the fact that he is not that important in the whole scheme of things and nothing about him is saved or redeemed or that he has just reached his end.

I read in one of Wayne Dyer's books that "We are a not a human being having a spiritual experience, rather we are a spiritual being having a human experience."

At the time, I thought that was quite profound and I liked it. It kind of made sense to me and was to have a profound effect on my beliefs. Again, an example of "There is no such thing as coincidence."

It was shortly after I had finished reading his book and I was selling long term care insurance that I was coming from a community called "The Villages" outside the city of Leesburg, Florida. Now there were two routes I could use to go home to Orlando. One was the Florida Turnpike and the other was an old, what I call a residential highway, State Road 441. At the fork in the road, I had to make a decision as to which way I was going to go. I chose Hwy. 441.

As I veered to the left, there was a light I had to stop at and the car in front of me, which was at least ten to fifteen years old and pretty beat up, had a bumper sticker on its rear bumper that read, "We are a not a Human Being having a Spiritual Experience, rather we are a Spiritual Being having a Human Experience."
I had never seen one before, and I have never seen one since, and this is now going on seven years. I wanted to stop him but never got the chance. If I had made the choice of taking the turnpike, I would never have seen it.

Considering what my beliefs are, the quote made a lot of sense to me. And the timing of that occurrence couldn't have been more fortuitous for me. It just seemed to validate what I was learning and believed in at a time in my life where reinforcement and validation was necessary. That brings me to my theory based upon the logic that I have been able to discern from my own life and the events that have occurred during my time on this plane of existence.

Can we agree at this point that this Universe is finitely balanced? Can we agree by definition that you are a Miracle and that you can perform miracles?

I joke that the Creator made a mistake and that we should have been born at 99 years old, and we should have worked backwards. This way when we are in our forties and thirties and twenties, we have all this experience and knowledge and now we have the physical bodies, energy and stamina to take advantage of it all. That would be true if all that knowledge and experience truly did go to waste. It doesn't.

Here I need you to bear with me while I explain something that I believe in because it seems to fit the pattern along with everything else. It may be a little hard to swallow at first and will again definitely cause some people to swallow deeply and probably will be appalled.

It is inconceivable to me to believe that all the knowledge we acquire and the experiences we live through and learn from simply disappear when we die and leave this plane of existence. All this knowledge we have accumulated is just, "poof", gone. Based upon what is known about the Universe we live in, that is incomprehensible.

So I offer you a theory to ponder. I say a theory because there is no proof of what happens to us when we die. There are only theories. If you believe in a man named John Edwards who claims he has connected with and communicated with those who have passed on, then this is easy to believe. If you do not believe in him or that people like him do exist and have never heard of him, then this will be new for you.

It has been stated scientifically that "thought" is energy. It is also scientifically stated that energy cannot die; therefore, thoughts cannot die. If that is true, where do they go? It is believed by some that the thoughts that we have end up in an aura of space, and anyone can tap into those thoughts at any given time. This translates to that you and someone in India, China or any other part of the world can end up thinking the same thing and can send thoughts back and forth across space to one another. The only thing is that none of you will know it or realize it unless you have had communication prior to or afterwards.

I know that you have heard of mental telepathy. That, as I am sure you know, is sending and/or receiving the thoughts of another person. You can be in the same room or different countries. It makes no difference.

I believe that I have experienced and used mental telepathy. It can be as simple as when a phone rings and you know who it is before you answer it and considering today's technology, before you look at the caller ID.

There were two instances in my life where I specifically tried to communicate with someone telepathically. In both instances (this was in the early seventies before the advent of cell phones) I concentrated on mentally connecting with them to have them call me and within a specific time frame. In both cases, it was within the hour. One was my first wife, and one was a business associate of mine. In both cases they called, and I asked what made them call. In both cases they told me they were doing something else and thought of me and decided to give me a call. With my first wife we were both in New York. With the business associate, he was in New Jersey and I was in New York. Needless to say, it was eerie and almost scary. I have not tried it lately and, of course, with the advent of the cell phone it is not necessary to expend that much energy.

I want to digress for one moment and relate to you information on just how powerful thoughts can be. This is from an article in the Reader's Digest issue of January 2005. In it they tell of a man who was paralyzed and had an operation to implant a small sensor in his brain. The sensor is linked to a computer that allows him to write e-mail, play video games, change channels on his TV and open curtains, using only his thoughts.

As a result of experiments with monkeys, Richard Normann, a professor of bioengineering at the University of Utah, invented a sensor that detects neural activity in the brain, which led to the development of the BrainGate Neural Interface System. This system is now being used in clinical trial in humans.

Although FDA approval is still several years and several million dollars away, (good ole FDA!), this is the beginning of a New Age of Neurotechnology.

In another article in the February 2006 issue of Reader's Digest, they talk about psychic powers and a team put together by the CIA. This team was credited in fingering the mole, Aldrich Ames and his wife Maria seven years prior to their capture. But the most intriguing message from the article was this statement, "Yes, the average person can learn to develop his or her psychic skills. While we often hear that people must be 'gifted' to be psychic, nearly anyone who learns the right principles and works at it can develop this perceptual skill."

To me, it is an example of the advances being made and the things that are possible as we investigate and understand what the human brain and body are capable of, proving once again *The Miracle Is You.*

Now there are times, when suddenly and out of nowhere I will picture the face of a loved one who has passed on. It will be a total interruption of my thought process. I know it has happened to you, too. Why is that? I have had occurrences where I will be driving and my thought process is on anything but my driving and there is a curve in the road, or someone cuts me off or decides to make a turn in front of me with no signal and without looking or thinking I make a sudden movement to avoid them, and, fortunately, no one is next to me. When I look back through my rear view mirror, there are a bunch of cars behind me. Or I suddenly will come back to focus and adjust to the road. As I am looking back, I clearly will see a vision of my father or sister. Or I will have a little trembling in my body and then see a vision of them. Why is that?

It is also amazing that when we take our last breath and our soul leaves the body that has been housing it for oh so many years, we supposedly weigh the same before and after that moment. Why is that?

If we consider all of these events and the balance of the Universe as I described previously, our souls have to go somewhere. The knowledge that we have experienced and learned cannot just die. There has to be another plane of existence. Based upon my experience, I also have to conclude that those who pass on do have a way of communicating with us through our thought processes.

I had a nephew who died of a brain aneurysm in the Pacific Ocean at the age of 32. Christopher was on his honeymoon and had been married only three days. Needless to say, it was the ultimate shock. He was the son of my sister who was killed by an act of domestic violence many years prior, so part of the tragedy was that he was the only contact we had of her on this plane. While he was alive, we all felt (the family) that we still had a piece of her with us. The night I received notice of his death, I awoke in the middle of the night to a very clear vision of him and my sister in the ocean, and they were hugging and smiling. Why was that? What did it mean?

Obviously, I took it to mean that they were now together and they were all right. I also took it to mean that she was there when he died to ease the transition of crossing over to the next plane, or heaven, or the next dimension. Take your pick. The vision also gave me comfort to know that he and my sister were **Okay**. With that knowledge or belief, I was able to go on with my life. Do I miss them? Of course. But knowing they are all right was the key.

The grieving process for the loved ones left behind is always difficult. And when you are dealing with a mother grieving for the loss of a child, that process is, in my experience, never-ending. It is tough. While I have not lost a child and obviously I am not a mother, I can't begin to tell you what one must go through or what it feels like. The only consolation I can offer for that is that the life we have been given is precious, and we must live it to the fullest. Our experiences mold us to be the person we are. While I don't want to minimize or in anyway undermine that type of loss, we still must go on.

I know a woman from New York named Sandy who has lost two sons, one at age 9 to a tragic accident and one at age 42, which was also relatively suddenly. I could not find the words to console her. She is prone to tears and depression, which can often result in physical pain because of those deaths. Sandy is a devoted mother and has three other children, but the losses have taken hold of her life. All the counseling and medication and even the knowledge that her kids would still want her to go on with her life and be happy doesn't seem to resolve the grief that she goes through.

Time is a great healer of emotional wounds but still doesn't cure all ills of grief. In time, we begin to function normally again, but there are moments where we still remember fondly those who have passed on and the emotions hit us hard. I know I feel that with my sister and my nephew. I believe sometimes that it is easier for a man to deal with grief because of the way we are made. I know it is so much more difficult for a woman because of the attachment of having given life, especially if the loss is a life you have given birth to. But even so, one must go on. You still have so much to give and get with living. One can still cherish the enjoyments that life can offer. You are still needed and still important to the Universe and the people in it and are still a note in the Grand Symphony of life.

I did offer this prayer based upon my beliefs, which I believe can help to some degree.

Infinite power, Cosmic power, God of the Universe and within me (at this point I tap my chest where my heart is). I want to thank you for my life and the people in my life and for what I have and ask for your help, guidance and direction. I ask that the guides help me in dealing with and coping with the loss of _____ (the name of the deceased person) and give me the strength to continue to live a productive life and be a happy person in harmony with the Universe and at peace with myself. _____ (Name of deceased person) will always be in my heart, and I pray that wherever he/she is he/she is also at peace and happy. Thank You.

This is a prayer I recite daily and then pray for the people in my life. I also use it for the guidance and direction to bring to me the people I need to meet to achieve my goals or for anything else where I need to ask for the help or guidance from the Universe and my guides. I have used it simply to put me in a state of mind to write and accept the guidance and direction from my guides to do so.

I find it comforting and, whether you believe like I do or not, **believe this**: the prayer and utterance of the words described will at least put your thoughts and requests into your subconscious mind, which will then go to work to accomplish what you ask for. This is the way of the Universe we live in.

You see, I do believe that there is another place to go to after we leave this world. To me it is comforting and reassuring to believe that. What it is? How does it work? What happens after that? I don't know.

Some theorize that we are reincarnated at a later date. It makes sense to a point, but I must admit, I don't know. What are the requirements for reincarnation? I don't know. And do we get to pick when, where and with whom we are reincarnated. There is a theory that, not only are we reincarnated, but that when we come back, we actually select the parents we are to be born to. Now my first question was, why would anyone want to be born in a desolate, famine-ridden place like the wilds of Africa? The answer I got was to be the sacrifice to hopefully show the world the problems that are so prevalent there and to bring attention to those problems. They would then go back and have another chance at reincarnation.

I have to admit that is stretching things a bit, even for me. But here again, as far-fetched as it may seem, I do wonder. This whole process raises so many questions, and I have none of the answers. Nor am I in any hurry to find them out. You can play mental manipulation with this until you exhaust yourself. There is only one way to find out.

This is a certainty in my mind, and that is that there is something else beyond the traditional Heaven and hell that has been force fed to us for years. And, of course considering that I believe we have a "Loving God," there can be no Hell, so it must be what is termed Heaven that is available from a religious standpoint.

It is known that we only use a small percentage of the capacity of the intelligence that we were born with and the brainpower that we have. It is known that mental telepathy is a possible phenomenon and a tool of communication. There are too many incidents giving evidence to support that. We do know that there are people that have honed their psychic abilities. While they are not right all the time, the fact remains that they are right some of the time, and that is all that is necessary to prove that it does exist. It is also noted that *we all* have this ability. I am also sure that you have seen evidence of it and have had incidents where you have used those abilities and never realized it, nor did you associate that power to yourself. It is as simple as knowing something is going to happen before it does or, as I said before, as in picking up the phone knowing who is on the other end before he or she speaks. That is evidence that you have psychic ability. I know I have had instances of that ability but have never consciously attempted to use it on a regular basis.

I have to admit that, as I write this book, as it was with the novels I have written, I could not have told you at the beginning of the book what I was going to put in it. I wrote a murder mystery novel and did not know myself until half way through the book who the killer was or was going to be. I believe, as I said before, that I was guided as I was with this book. That means that each individual has spirit guides that are assigned to them; and if you are in tune to them and ask for their help, they *will* communicate through you and guide you as to what is right for you or assist you, especially in the creative process. Many songwriters will tell you the same thing. It just flows through you.

I am so often amazed at times at what I do write and what comes out of me. I am amazed at how I ever thought to put that in there. I also believe that these guides will change as you grow and your needs change. After all, there are billions of people who have passed on over the centuries of our existence, so I am sure there are enough to go around and then some, which is why I believe that there is and has to be something else after this life.

There is no doubt that all this deserves a whole lot more explanation and discussion, but the purpose of this exercise is to provoke thought and questions. Is it possible? Does it make any sense? The intention is for you to find your own answers and come to your own conclusions. I have offered mine and welcome any questions or comments you may have on this subject.

Considering all this, I have to conclude that there is something else. Everything in this Universe has cycles. The seasons, summer, spring, winter, fall and everything that revolves around those seasons. Even a woman has her menstrual cycle and cycle of fertility. Even the hurricanes and monsoons have their cycles. The whole Universe, as balanced as it is, is set up on cycles. So must human life and death be cyclical. So says Papa J.

CHAPTER TWENTY-ONE

EVERY DAY IS A GIFT

In the last chapter, I spoke of a woman named Sandy and the tragedy that had befallen her and her family. Well, I had met Sandy and her husband Bobby for dinner recently and had given her the two novels I had written as a gift and a token of friendship. We talked about her losses and the grief that she was dealing with.

The next day she called my wife Ellie and thanked me for the books. During the conversation she mentioned that she was looking for a bookmark to use as she read the books. She pulled one out of another book she had, and the following saying was written on it, "Every day is a gift." This phrase seemed to strike a note within her, and she took great comfort in the phrase and from the timing in finding it. The phrase struck a note within me, too, and I decided it would make a great subtitle for a chapter.

Now as I have said before, ***"There is no such thing as coincidence,"*** and I believe this was supposed to happen just as it did. I just hope it helps her deal with her losses because it is true. ***Every day IS a Gift.***

We use such phrases as; "One day at a time." "Tomorrow is promised to no one." "Live each day as it comes." "Live for today." How true they all are. Now let's add, "Every day is a gift."

I mentioned my friend Richard in a previous chapter. He recently had radical surgery for his third bout with cancer, which took thirteen and a half hours. He will be coming home today and will adjust to his new way of life. Considering what he has gone through and survived, I wondered what his state of mind would be. I thought surely that he would be so thankful to just be alive and found out that wasn't the case, initially.

It is difficult adjusting your life to having a colostomy bag and a urine bag attached to your body. Your system is constantly unloading waste, and you never know when it will fill up and need to be changed. You need to learn how to replace them and make sure they don't leak. You are conscious of the odors coming from them. It will take some time to get his system regulated so he can consider something as simple as going out to dinner.

I asked him if he knew what he knows now would he have had the surgery, and his response was, "No." I asked if he will do what is necessary to adjust to his situation, and he said, "Yes" And then he added, "See me in two or three months."

We all make choices throughout our life. Sometimes those choices are as monumental as to whether to live or to die. Every time we make a decision, though, there are always consequences, sometimes good sometimes difficult. Richard's decision was to have the surgery and live. Is he sorry he chose that? My indication is that the jury is still out.

I asked him if he *sees* the world any differently, and his response was, "I don't see anything. Right now all I care about is to get my life straightened out and find out what I need to do to get on with whatever quality of life I will be able to have with this situation."

I honestly thought his outlook would be different, but then I am not the one who went through four years of fighting cancer. I am not the one who is now in pain and constant discomfort having to adjust to a situation that really digs deep into the quality of life one can have. It limits what you can do and where you can go. For someone who thought nothing of packing up on short notice and taking a weekend trip or traveling to places throughout the country and the world, he is now unable to do that. For one who enjoyed sitting at the pool in his bathing suit soaking up the rays of the sun at his timeshare in Cancun and listening to classical music and opera through his headphones, this is a shock at being so restricted. Being unable to sit for any length of time (even a half-hour) is unsettling. I can understand how one may question, "What did I do?"

It seems the fight has taken a toll on my friend. It seems that his will to live may be weakening. Since I believe that there is something else after this life, and as much as I truly thank my Creator for my life, the people in it and for what I have, I have to admit, I don't know if I would have gone through all that.

I believe in quality of life, and while I am in no hurry to cross over to the next plane of existence and will not go without a fight, I question whether I would go through what he did. There is no guarantee for him, nor for anyone else for that matter, as to how much longer he is going to live. The prognosis is vague. I have heard two or three years. I have heard eight to ten years. Ten years would put him at 78. To me, at this stage of my life that is an age I would be satisfied with. Two or three years I don't know. That is a blink of an eye in retrospect, especially living with a limited quality of life.

Richard is a very, very good friend, and I hurt for him. I also hurt for his wife, Mary Price, and hate the thought of her losing him. I want to see him have a new outlook on life. I want him to live every day and *see* it as a gift. I want him to feel that a breath of fresh air is a gift to him. Being out and seeing the sun and not through a window is a gift for him. Hugging and kissing his devoted wife is a gift for him because he was not sure he would ever do that again. Seeing and hugging his two daughters is a gift for him. Being back in his home and his own bed. Seeing friends and well-wishers and all the people who prayed for him. Driving a car again. Going to bed each night and looking forward to waking up the next day. Just living the day and whatever it brings is a gift for him, and I want him to thank his Creator every day for that "GIFT."

Alas, I have no answer here. I know that what I want for him doesn't matter. While I love him and love having him around, I truly pray that he be happy and, above all, I pray that he finds peace, whatever and wherever that may be for him.

An update on Richard: his attitude is improving and he is adjusting slowly and getting back to being the cantankerous loving soul that I knew him to be.

When you look at a situation like Richard's and put your life in perspective, don't we have a lot to be thankful for? Yet we really don't do that. We go to work on Monday and can't wait until Friday. We look forward to our weekend. We practically wish away the precious days we have on this earth. What a shame. What a waste of such precious time.

It may sound a bit ridiculous to you. Maybe even a bit Pollyanna. But shouldn't we be thankful we are alive and for the quality of life we have? Shouldn't we be thankful for our families? That we have a job to go to? Shouldn't we be thankful that we have the ability to go to a job and the health to perform whatever it is that we do? How about that we have food on our table and a roof over our head?

When you stop to think about it, we have a lot to be thankful for, like all those little things that we take for granted. No we may not have everything that we want, but we surely have a lot more than most. And if you have love in your life and in your heart, you are also more fortunate than many. We need to celebrate this Gift every day that has been given to us. We must thank our Creator for giving us this day each and every day.

Am I preaching? You bet! This is where your 20 minutes a day comes in. This is where you take the opportunity for not only reflecting on yourself but to be thankful for all that you do have in your life. This is where you *SEE* what transpired in that day and appreciate the *Miracle of Life* and the *Miracle that is you*. And then thank your *GOD* and ask for a tomorrow. Ask for another Gift.

If you will do this, you will begin to look upon your life differently. You will begin to enjoy it more while you still can. You will find in retrospect of the day that those problems you had that day really didn't amount to that much and, better still, you got through them all and it wasn't really that bad. In fact, you will find more good things than bad that occurred during the day if you look hard enough.

Your outlook, your attitude and your life will change for the better. You will truly *SEE* that *"Every day IS a gift."* I promise you. So says Papa J.

CHAPTER TWENTY-TWO

EXAMPLES OF THE MIRACLE

It was difficult to select the examples of the Miracle of the Human Spirit and those who gave back to society and to others less fortunate or who overcame physical handicaps or, to me, exemplified the type of an individual I would want my kid to grow up to be like. There really are so many examples of people I have met in my lifetime that I just decided to pick the ones who stood out for me. The celebrities I have chosen, while I don't know them personally, their stories and personalities, achievements and courage touched me.

One of the best examples I know of who exemplifies the possibilities of what one can achieve coming from nothing is Oprah Winfrey. Here is a black woman who brought herself up from the depths of poverty to become one of the most famous women on our planet. She is a prime example of what an individual can do not only for herself but how one person can change the world and the lives of so many people.

Yes, she is one of the richest people in the world, but so much more than that. She gives back to humanity. The way she gives of herself as well as her money is something to be proud of and to honor.

I realize as I write this about her, I don't know her, never met her and I really don't know anything about her life other than what I might read in a book or magazine, or what I might see and hear in an interview she has given.

But I do know she climbed her ladder of success with grit and determination and never forgot how she got there. Yes, she had help and, yes, she got her chances, but she did so because of her attitude and working within the framework of the Creator's Universe. The people she needed to meet and know to assist her in her climb were brought to her by her wanting it and by believing in herself. Her legacy is the example of a person who had the courage and faith to step out and make it happen. She was a black woman in a white man's world, and she beat the odds and made her mark in one of the toughest venues to do so: daytime television.

She opened doors for other women in general as well as other black women. And she continues to give back to her people as well as people from all races. Most of it you never hear about. She is an amazing example of what can be accomplished working with the Creator and the Universe we live in and deserves every accolade and award that can be bestowed upon her. God has not only blessed Oprah Winfrey but has blessed us with her presence in our generation.

Lance Armstrong is another example of what the human spirit can accomplish and achieve. He beat cancer and then won the toughest and most grueling bicycle race, the "Tour de France," an unprecedented seven times. And he, too, gives back and has established a foundation to help others. He continuously gives of himself and his time to fund that foundation and keep it running. Yes, with each race he won there was a team that helped him. Again he drew to him the people he needed to accomplish an unprecedented goal, one I doubt will be matched for many generations to come.

No one does it alone. Everyone needs help. That is why it is so important to work within the framework of the Universe and our Creator. So you, too, can draw to you the people you need to assist you in achieving your goals.

These are two examples of people of notoriety who in my opinion stand out far above many others. There are also people who are not famous that give of themselves and back to the community that they reside in: the people who help out at your place of worship, the people who help out at chartable functions and events, the people who volunteer at our schools and at our hospitals and nursing homes. All these people give back and should proudly give themselves a great pat on the back.

There is another person I would like to mention in this category, and since it is my book, I will do so, and that is my wife Ellie. And I do so for this one reason. Until I met Ellie, I have never met a person who did not have one mean bone in her body. This woman is never, ever vindictive. However angry she gets, she will not strike back to hurt you. She will take the insult and hurt inside rather than strike back in kind. She is truly a "good" person with a very warm and pleasant personality. She has been the caregiver for both her parents as well as her brother and has handled a fulltime job and a family while doing so. Now I am not saying that she is the only one to ever do that, and I am sure that there are many people who probably have done as much and a lot more. But she is MY wife and I believe that she deserves to be recognized for being the type of person who exemplifies the Miracles you can perform just by being yourself and the loving, caring, sweet person you naturally are. She has also been an inspiration to me as well as my life mate. She is what makes everything I do worthwhile. I guess I would say she makes me whole and complete.

Two other people I am going to mention are people who, despite physical handicaps, are productive members of society. The first is the man who does my website, my book covers and helps me with computer problems when I screw up. That is Scott Cleary who was born with Arthrogryposis, a rare congenital disorder that is characterized by reduced mobility of the joints and dislocation of the hips. While it deforms his body, his mind is sharp and his determination to lead a full and productive life overcoming his physical handicap is, in my mind, miraculous. He is an inspiration to me and is an example of what the human spirit can accomplish and overcome.

He is also an example of the Universe bringing to me the people I need to meet to achieve my goals. Scott is the fiancé of a lady that I work with. Margaret and I have worked together for a few years, and she, too, is a sweetheart of a person. It wasn't until we both won a trip to New York as top producers for Blue Cross Blue Shield of Florida that I found out about the talents that Scott had. He is now an integral part of my team. So, you see, I promise you the system does work.

Another is a man who works for the same company as I, Donald, who lost both legs. Yet he manages to navigate his way to a job, has a family and is a productive member of society. I couldn't conceive of having to deal with that situation and question if I would have the guts to do so. He is another miracle in my world.

Now what problems they have and deal with on a daily basis I can only guess. But the fact that they have both made the conscious decision to not allow their physical handicaps to limit them is to me a Miracle.

Each and every one of those people have and are performing miracles in so much as they are responsible for changing someone's life for that moment by their efforts.

Understand the effect you can have and do have on other people and *see* the effect you can have on others as well as the effect others have on you and you will learn a great deal about yourself and the Universe you live in. You will also begin to understand what I have said here and what this life is all about. I promise you it will work for you, too. So says Papa J.

CHAPTER TWENTY-THREE

HAPPINESS

We know that time does not stand still for anyone. Days, weeks, months, years pass, and we get older. Hopefully we have lived that time and used it well. Hopefully we have learned from our experiences and learned well. Hopefully we have enjoyed the time and the years we have spent living our life. If we have, then we are happy.

It doesn't pay to look back with regret as we connect the dots. We can't change anything in our past anyway. But we can learn from it, and, therefore, the exercise is worth doing. But don't waste time and energy by dwelling on past mistakes.

Happiness is also state of mind, as is abundance. It is up to you to be happy. ***It is your job to be happy.*** The old saw that the "glass is half full or half empty" is a truism that can rule your life. It is all how you look at it.

One chooses to be happy. You were put on this earth to be happy. It is a matter of being content with: who you are, the people in your life, the job you have, the house you live in, the amount of money you have, the wife and family that you have. If you are not content with those things, take your time and change them, one and all.

We have touched on many subjects and, hopefully, have come to many realizations as you have passed through this book. The one constant has always been that, ***it is up to you***. It is all your choice. It took me a long time to learn that. I pray it doesn't take you as long.

I am a happy man because of what I have learned, and I now know that I know that I know. I am a happy man as I watch the miracle of life unfold and the effect it has on the lives of the people around me. The fact that I can teach others what I have learned and can and do enjoy my life, the people in it and what I have.

That doesn't mean that I don't have a bad day. It doesn't mean that I don't lose my cool. It doesn't mean that I live a perfect life.

I still get road rage when someone cuts me off or goes so slow that time seems to stand still. Remember: I live in Florida, the home of the retiree, where the state flag shows a picture of two hands and a forehead protruding above a steering wheel. My kids, my wife, my co-workers, the company I work for can still tick me off. My aches and pains still bother me, as I grow older. But, all in all, I really am a very fortunate and happy man.

I have wealth that money can't buy. A roof over my head, money in the bank and Lord knows I eat well and whatever I choose to eat. And I have my writing, which keeps my mind sharp and gives me a satisfaction that is the ultimate. Now add to all that grandchildren who are a tremendous source of pride and unconditional love. What more can a man can ask for and along with that, the opportunity to teach them about this glorious Universe we live in? Why wouldn't I be happy?

Now you have to do it for yourself. You have to find that "thing," your purpose in this life that you want to do. Whatever it is that gives you that warm feeling in the pit of your stomach and then pushes its way up through your gut to create a smile on your face and warm feeling in your heart, you have to find your purpose for being here. I believe I have given you some direction and a method on how to succeed and bring to you the people you need to meet and know once you have determined what your purpose is.

Where did you come from? I think that was answered pretty clearly. Why are you here? You are here to learn about the workings of our Universe. Then to teach what you learn to others and to live and enjoy the life you have been given. Who are you? *The Miracle Is You.* You have within you the power to create your own little world where life works for you. The Universe wants you to have it. Now you have to find it. It is there, waiting for you. *Go Grab It. Go Love It. Go Live It.*

This is such an awesome Universe. There is so much that is available to you. There is so much you can do to be a part of it. It comes down to just being you. You don't have to be a saint, or a millionaire, or this famous person of worldwide notoriety. You just have to be you. And be the best you that you can be. It's really not that difficult.

Let me leave you with a little quiz as an illustration of how important you can be to an individual and how important other individuals have been to you.

1. Name the five wealthiest people in the world
2. Name the last five Heisman trophy winners
3. Name the last three winners of the Miss America Pageant.
4. Name three people who have won the Nobel Prize and for what.
5. Name the last three; best actors, best actresses and best pictures that won Academy Awards.

Now part two of the quiz.

1. Name three teachers who helped you through school.
2. Now three friends who have been there for you in a time of stress or trouble.
3. Name three people who have taught you something worthwhile. (parents are allowed)
4. Name three people who made you feel special.

5. Think of five people you enjoy spending time with.

The lesson here is; the people who actually make a difference in your life and have had the most positive effect on your life, are not the richest, the most famous, the ones getting all the press and who have won these distinguished awards. They are the people who have demonstrated that they care about you and have tried to help you and support you.
This philosophy was attributed to Charles Schultz the cartoonist who created the Peanut's characters.

It has also been mine for many years. It's us, what I call the "Little People" that actually make this world "go" and keeps it going. It's *You* being the best *You* that you can be that will and does make a difference.

You are special. You are great. We have proven that because you can perform miracles by changing peoples' lives, even for just a moment. And that moment can be a year, a day or just a few seconds. But you have changed that person's life, and the memory of what you did will stay with him or her forever. Think of that: You have had an effect on someone that will stay in his or her memory bank forever. What an awesome feat. That is a miracle!

Remember: You are a note in the Grand Symphony of life. You have the power. Think of the serenity prayer.

God grant me the serenity to accept the things I cannot change, the courage to change the things I can and the wisdom to know the difference.

Well, you have been provided the wisdom to know the difference. You can control only your life: who you are, what you think and what you do. Everything else is out of your control. So now make the changes necessary for you. Have the courage to make those changes. *See* and be aware of what's around you: people, places, things. *Live* your life the way you want it to be. You can do it. And the only person you need do it for is *you*. The byproduct of doing that will have the positive and desired effect on everyone else in your life. So you do it for you, and all else will simply fall into place. After all, **The Miracle Is You. So says Papa J.**

If this book changes the life of one person and allows or inspires him or her to find his or her purpose in this life, then he or she will change another. I have dropped my pebble in the lake. Are you one of the ripples?

P.S. after over 50 years it has been two months that I have not smoked. I believe this time I will make it. Godspeed and God bless to all.

You Can Contact "Papa J" at www.HouseofPapaJ.com

POEMS

BY

JEFFREY J. HALPERIN

AKA

PAPA J

Jeffrey J. Halperin

TO MY FRIEND GENNARRO

As we travel the paths of life
Through the trials and through the strife
Many places people and things
Become a part of what life brings

We remember some and yet
Many others we soon forget
Sometimes by choice we let them pass
Some, of times that did not last

But then there's some I don't know why
Through quirks of fate will just drop by
No real purpose or mission sent
They just appear without pretense

They date your life and bring to you
Their late events and share what's new
But never fail in their own way
They bring a smile and make your day

They touch that place inside of you
That seems to let a light shine through
Your head comes clear, the mist abates
And suddenly you just feel great

Troubles are gone, they've lost their sting
He lifts you up, again you're King
This person is a friend by name
Whatever his, it's all the same

I do believe a friend like this
Is born to share his special gift
May even be he doesn't know
The good he does and all he sows

Gennaro, my friend, I cannot tell
The many times you cast your spell
And helped me through a time of stress
Inspiring words with cheerfulness

And if it's true that we come back
Your future life will never lack
I only hope, again one day
When we come back, you'll come my way
With deep affection and best wishes, Jeff

Jerry was a friend who would come by my place of business
on occasion, totally unplanned, and we would talk about
many things. The most amazing thing is that, regardless of
my attitude at the time, I was always feeling up and
positive after one of his visits. He was a special person
and friend.

Jeffrey J. Halperin

THE FRIENDSHIP

Friendship is a fragile thing
a different kind of love
it can build as years go by
or get lost in changing times

If it survives the test of time
the bond created through thick and thin
creates an identity all its own
it sings to the world with its own voice

this entity revels in the successes
and shares in the joys of its life
it too feels the hurt and the pain
it encounters along the journey

While we have never really spoken of it
I want you to know, as we reach this crossroad
the many joys this entity has brought to my life
the knowledge I have gained through it

The example of you I have looked up to,
not without human flaws, but the courage,
and fortitude, under duress, you have displayed,
not just now, but all through the years.

I extol the entity which has allowed me
to be who I am, and who accepted me
with my human frailties and flaws
and never judged my actions or misdeeds

I have tried in my own way to contribute
as much as I have been blessed to receive
to make this entity as enriching for you
as much as it has brought to my life

I almost believe that our spirits go back
before this life and beyond this life
that this entity was created and born
so that we may meet and nourish it
which seems to indicate it will flourish
and continue to grow for many life years
because there is so much more we must
experience and live and share.

Only now we are aware of it
now we will cherish it even more
now we know why we have it
now we know how precious it is

Now we must glean from it
the joys and the laughter
now we must celebrate
with the voracity of Leos

Now this entity comes to fore
and through the God within each of us
we will pray at the table of friendship
and we will once more conquer adversity, with love.

Fear not my friend, love jeff

This was originally written for my friend Richard Eckstein, and on occasion I have found cause to modify it and send it to other people that I believe it can apply to. In its essence it applies to many of my friends.

Jeffrey J. Halperin

THROUGH THE EYES OF A CHILD
By Jeffrey J. Halperin 7/2000-10/2005

I look at the sky, and what do I see
The moon, the stars, the whole galaxy
I look at the sea, so deep and so blue
The tide takes the old, and brings in the new

I see mountains, so huge and so high
Tips capped with snow, reach to the sky
'Tis our Universe, in all of its splendor
Viewing all this, I start to wonder?

The sounds of buses, of cars and of trains
Horns that go beep, the roar of the planes
Birds that are chirping, motors are roaring
Choirs are singing, drills that are boring
The din, the clamor, of day and of night
I hear the voices, the voices of life

I smell the flowers, the grass after rain
Salt air from the sea, a field growing grain
The taste of a spice, good cheese and good wine
Just like us humans, improving with time

God's Universe, is ours to enjoy
To nurture and guard, not rape and destroy
Please listen and learn, you've gone astray
God sent me to you, to show you the way

Give me this moment, put your hand in mine
Let me be your guide, free up your mind
Your heart, it's so cold, where mine is so warm
No need to worry, I mean you no harm

I want you to see, to smell and to hear
To taste and to feel, to love and not fear

I am called child, I love by design
I know not of fear, of hate nor of crime
I thrill to your touch, your love and your kiss
I unencumbered, live only in bliss

You have been tainted, frustrations abound
You no longer see, you've lost what you found
It's still, all right here, see past life's disguise
Just look at the world, through this child's eyes.

I strongly believe adults don't learn enough from the children, especially when it comes to seeing what's around them and the purity with which a child sees you and the Universe we live in.

Printed in the United States
49074LVS00006B/154-255